HARMONY, LIGHTNESS AND HORSES

Integrating Body and Mind to Ride Your Horse

Ylvie Fros

Published by "The Art of Riding by Ylvie Fros"
www.artofriding.org
www.ylviefros.nl

First edition

ISBN: 978-90-829404-0-4

Layout Design by Fenke Fros
Illustrations copyright ©2017, 2018 Christine Leemans
Chapter illustrations SveslaTasla/shutterstock.com
Cover illustration AnfisaFocusova/shutterstock.com
Back cover illustration copyright © Fenke Fros
Photographs copyright ©2016, 2017, 2018 Maybel van der Linden
Photographs copyright ©2012 Janneke Koekhoven
Photographs AbramovaKseniya/shutterstock.com
Used by permission. All rights reserved.

"As a horse trainer and instructor, I live to develop my mind, my body and the mind and body of my horses. I am passionate about passing on my knowledge and experience to other horse lovers so that we can keep our horses happy and healthy, and together send positive energy into this world."

This book is for my horses, my greatest teachers

Acknowledgments

So many great instructors, colleagues and friends have helped me gather all the knowledge and experiences that resulted in the blog articles that became this book. I have studied horseback riding since I was a child and have ventured through most of the mainstream disciplines, where I met many inspiring people along the way. My rescue horses showed me the way toward the Academic Art of Riding. In this discipline, I learned to understand horse biomechanics and sound (classical) dressage training to help improve my horses' bodies and minds. And I developed an interest in moving beyond the mechanical, into the realm of art and true connection.

To understand the mind-body connection of the rider, I studied – and am still studying – Centered Riding®, Martial Arts, the Alexander Technique, Zentherapy® and am currently working as both a riding teacher/clinician and a bodyworker to assist riders in releasing both emotional and physical trauma, loosen stuck tissue and become more free, stable and flexible both on and off the horse.

While preparing this book I have gained so many valuable insights from so many people that it is perhaps unavoidable that I will forget to give credit to some. However, a few people really stand out; those who have mentored me for many years, who have been sparring partners in my quest, and have provided me with such valuable feedback and insights, that without them these thoughts would never have found their way onto paper.

Among them is my patient teacher in the Academic Art of Riding, Bent Branderup, who was the first to explain to me clearly how correct dressage exercises arise from correct biomechanics. As I continue to train for him, I am still amazed by the wealth of knowledge Bent possesses; from the history of riding, to biomechanics and the lineages of old baroque horse breeds. His eye for detail and his never-ending thirst for more knowledge are a great inspiration.

This book would never have become what is it today without my friend and mentor Tom Nagel, who taught me that how bodies work off the horse is how they work on the horse. I am most thankful that Tom introduced me to the world of Zen and bodywork.

And Karen Irland, Level IV Centered Riding® instructor, I thank her for helping me find the connections between classical riding, the biomechanics of the horse and the biomechanics of the rider. But most of all for showing me the example of a truly centered teacher who lives by the concept 'less is more.' I have never seen anyone carrying the energy of a full clinic group with so much intent and so few words.

Then there are my many friends and colleagues in Centered Riding®, Zen, bodywork, the martial arts and the Academic Art of Riding by Bent Branderup®, with whom I have trained, shared ideas and shared laughter and pain during this journey, and who hopefully will continue to do so for a very long time. And of course my many horses and students, who asked questions, were available for my experiments, provided feedback and trusted me to assist them and learn from them on their own individual journeys. I cannot begin to express my gratitude for having met these special people and horses, for the trust they gave me, and all the lessons they taught me.

A special thanks to Nicole Lariviere for her help with developing Centered Groundwork. And last but not least, to Yanick, for supporting me many years in my horse studies and never complaining about all the hours I spent on my own development.

I thank you all from the bottom of my heart.

Contents

The Biomechanics and Training of the Horse

Foreword by Bent Branderup

What is the "Art" in the Academic Art of Riding? For me, riding is only art, when two spirits want to do, what two bodies can. From experience I can tell, that it is seldom the horses body or mind that sets the limits. The limits on your journey to the Academic Art of Riding that hold you back from being the best rider you can be, are the limits of your own body and mind. If you decide to become a traveller on the way to the Academic Art of Riding, you decide to challenge yourself in order to move your own boundaries so you can be in a better contact to your horse.

Ylvie Fros has been my student for many years now and she is one of the licensed Bent Branderup® Trainers. She is a dedicated rider and trainer and has been experimenting with different approaches that can help riders to master the challenges they face on their journey to the Art. A rider who gets stuck on his journey will often find the solution in a change of perspective. Ylvie has been experimenting with different approaches in teaching and coaching humans on their way to the Academic Art of Riding. This book gives insight, how Zen, Centered Riding and the Academic Art of Riding can give guidance in order to develop a better connection between the human and the horse. The purpose of art is not to make an ideal become perfect reality, but to enlighten reality.

-Bent Branderup-

Introduction

My initial plan was to write a book about the seat of the rider. An anatomical and technical guide for riders, explaining the correct way to use and move your body. But in the course of my own development in riding and while writing my blog posts, I realized that, yes, while the technique and anatomy behind a good seat is very important to know, in the end it is not theoretical knowledge that makes you a good rider; it is the good use of your body and mind that does. Without the right mindset and intent, your body will not do what you ask it to do. A mind that is in the moment and allows you to feel will benefit you far more when you are around horses compared to an over-thinking, analytical brain that blocks out all signals from your body.

They say that you can only teach what you know. I believe you can only teach what you have truly experienced. There is a massive difference between knowing something and having experienced it. Riding is all about experiences. Theoretical understanding is important, but there are many good trainers out there who can teach you about the techniques of dressage exercises, which muscles to train and why. Also, some great trainers out there do a fantastic job teaching people about rider biomechanics. Many books have been written about these subjects. But you still have to go out and collect your own experience beyond this theoretical knowledge.

The experience that I try to pass on to my students, and through my blog posts and this book to all of you riders out there, is that it requires training of both mind and body to become the best rider you can be. There are things you need to understand, things you need to feel and things you need to experience in order to develop. The connection and integration of your body and mind so that they work as one is what most of us have lost and what eastern philosophies such as Zen teach you to re-find.

I will give you a variety of ideas on how you can work on your body and your mind. With the ultimate goal to become free of fear, pain, stress and negative beliefs and to improve balance, stability, freedom of movement, patience, awareness and upright posture while being with your horse(s). By developing our own bodies and minds we will be able to help our horses to carry us in harmony and lightness, with joy and mutual understanding.

This book is not a 'how-to' book in the usual sense. It does not tell you how to train the shoulder-in, how to train collection or how to do a flying change. It does not even tell you how you should handle your horse. But it does tell you what you can work on in your own body and how you can train your mind in order to improve your riding and your relationship with your horse. It gives you some ideas to try out on your horse. But this book is not meant to give you a complete structure or overview of a riding 'method'.

Instead of a practical step-by-step guide on how to use your body and aids, this book is a collection of thoughts, ideas and experiences that will give you various perspectives on the same topics: the body and mind of the horse rider. This collection may alter, expand and be revised as time goes by. With each new experience, my riding and teaching evolves. As do my thoughts about riding.

Happy reading!

- Ylvie

THE RIDER'S MIND

The Power of Samadhi: Ride in the Space between Your Thoughts

My training is in the Art of Riding, which is in fact the art of becoming one with the body and soul of another being – the horse – and through that connection, to become one with the entire universe. To experience that there are no borders between one being and the other, no limit between where your body and mind ends and where your horse's body and mind begins. To find that state of body and mind in which energy can flow limitlessly between you and your horse and to maintain that delicate equilibrium in which there are no thoughts, no judgments and no ego, that is what my training is all about. I train to ride in what my teacher Tom Nagel calls the 'space between my thoughts'. Our horses are always in that state, waiting for us to meet them there.

Before we can reach that level of riding in which we flow from one step to the next without thinking, analyzing and judging, there has to be another level of training: the training of techniques. In this stage, which is really just the beginning of things, we have to learn how our body and the body of the horse functions by studying biomechanics and anatomy and by training technical movements such as the shoulder-in and the haunches in. We study how to use the seat, legs and reins for all exercises. Most riders stop their training there or continue to pursue techniques on higher and higher levels of exercises. However, if we stay on the level of analyzing our exercises, of riding in a technical way, we will not develop on the level where the real magic happens. We will not develop true art.

I like this example that my trainer Bent Branderup uses in his theory lectures. First, you are a beginner who learns a handcraft: the basic techniques. When you control the craft you can become a master. And some masters become true artists. But you cannot become an artist if you do not master the tools and techniques to create your art. An artist also needs to have some feeling for harmony and emotional expression. Artists use their tools to express or arouse feelings. Without feelings, there is no true art. And also, without the basic handcraft, the techniques, you cannot create the art to express yourself and these feelings.

After you have learned some basic techniques and skills in riding horses, the next level is where we sometimes, maybe even by accident, experience a deeper connection with our horses. On this level we notice that just by thinking about an exercise, our body and the body of the horse respond and make it happen. Our technique has become automatic, without conscious thinking. Instead of our analyzing mind, our bodies start riding the horse. We experience instead of analyze. We feel instead of think. We move from handcraft to art. This does not need to happen on a high level of riding. It can happen on your basic circle in walk. Wherever you master the technique, you can start to create art. Everything new you learn will bring you first back to the level of cognitive learning, of mastering the techniques and understanding the exercises. Only after you have mastered the technique in that new exercise can you feel that flow of energy again and allow the exercise to happen naturally.

The final level is where we can remain in this state of non-doing for longer and longer. In Zen, this is called Samadhi. We not only feel the connection with our horse but through this connection we become more aware of the world around us. We hear background sounds, like cars passing by and the birds in the trees, and these sounds become a part of us. We feel the rain or the sunshine and make it part of us without it affecting us. We feel the horse under us but we also become the horse and the horse becomes part of us. We experience a stillness inside, that allows us to connect with the universe on a deeper level. We become one with our horse. This is often described as the 'centaur feeling'. The mythological creature that is half man-half horse. However, I would say we don't become anything and we definitely do not give up half of our being. The experience for me is more that we stop being anything. We just are. One. Nothing. In Samadhi this is the same. On this level there are no bad rides or good rides. Bad and good are judgments and there are no judgments here. It is just what it is. In this state, we experience true harmony. And it doesn't stop with the horse, it encompasses everyone and everything around us. In this state, all I feel is a deep love and compassion for everything and an intense joy in being part of it all. In this state, I let go of all technique and use my body without any conscious thinking. And then, everything works, everything flows and I

experience a quality and energy like nothing else. My horse is floating, our breathing becomes one, I feel the joy in my horse and it becomes my joy. Our movements are one and we ride like magic.

This result, this ultimate feeling of being me, the horse, the universe and nothing at the same time, is the crown on the hard training. It is the result of the long journey of training the techniques (the handcraft) and the mind (the art). And at the same time it is the most humbling experience, which shows that you are still a beginner in the real art, which is to integrate this state of being in your life 24 hours a day. This is for me the true practice of Zen.

Before an artist can reach the highest level of artistic expression they must have learned some techniques and skills and by countless repetition and exercise must have perfected these skills to the point where their work can move up in the realm of art. This is the realm where the artist does not need to think about skills or techniques. Instead, they clear their mind of all thoughts and allow their breathing and body to move the tools and create. The clearer the artist's mind, the clearer they will bring an artistic creation into the world.

The same goes for us riders. The more we ride in this space between our thoughts, the more we let our bodies and aids flow from a clear and untroubled mind, the clearer the horses will follow our directions and the more all the movements will flow. This space between our thoughts is a form of Samadhi. We can still think, we can still visualize what we want to happen but our senses are heightened and we do not let any judgment or thought cloud our performance. We simply are. We, riders, create art that does not last. Every stride of the horse is a new creation, lasting only for the moment. We do not look back to enjoy or gloat over what we have produced, we do not fear or anticipate the steps yet to come. We ride every stride. One step at a time. And in this way, we find a harmony with our horse that lasts a moment and at the same time, an eternity.

It All Starts with Awareness

If we want to improve the use of our mind and body during riding, it starts with awareness. Aa a rider, you need to be aware of what you are thinking, feeling and doing while being up there on your horse and you need to be aware of what your horse is doing, thinking and feeling underneath you. When you ride, ask yourself some questions: Are you aware that both your hips are moving separately from each other? Is the movement in both hips symmetrical? Can you feel your breathing change when you transition up or down? How do you feel when your approach that jump? Do you believe you will make it over or are you afraid your horse will take the bar down? Can you feel the tension or relaxation in your horse's back? Can you feel your horse's hind legs? Can you sense whether he is enjoying himself?

It is important to observe your body and your thoughts while you ride. Quite often, riders are so busy doing things to their horses and giving aids and putting their horses in a frame that they pay little to no attention to themselves. And if the attention gets turned toward themselves a little, it often focuses on what their body is doing wrong. Instead, I recommend you first start to feel what your body is doing right and where you can feel movement in your body. Start by allowing each body part to be moved by your horse. Can you consciously allow your ankles, knees, hips, spine, arms and head to be moved by your horse's movement?

Then observe your thoughts: what do you think about while riding? Are you distracted, thinking about your grocery list or the incident you just had at work? Or can you be fully in the 'now', together with your horse? Do you think more negative or more positive thoughts? Are these thoughts about your horse or about you? Stop thinking anything negative about yourself or about your horse. Instead, focus on what is going right and what you and your horse can do together. You may need to adjust your goals and be happy with smaller things.

A good way to start to feel what is happening and to connect with your horse is to do this very simple exercise: Ask someone to take your horse

by the rein and gently walk it around the riding arena. Get your feet out of your stirrups, let your legs hang down and if you are comfortable; close your eyes. Don't judge what you feel, and don't do anything. Just be soft and passive and allow the horse to move you and allow your body to be moved. Feel what is there: can you feel your hips moving? Can you feel your legs swinging? Can you feel the movement travel up your spine and leaving your body out the top of your head? Can you feel your head moving? Can you feel your own and your horse's breathing? Can you feel your own body and the horse's body move together? Then open your eyes. Does that change anything? How does the visual part of your brain influence your feeling? Our ultimate goal is to have this feeling of togetherness all the time. To have body and mind become one, and to have horse and rider become one. In the end, two minds and two bodies becoming as one. The ultimate Centaur.

The key to this togetherness is not technique. It is not about doing. It is about being in the here and now and allowing your body and mind and the body and mind of your horse to flow. Technique helps to direct that flow. Body awareness and training will help refine it. The education and physical development of your horse and yourself will allow this togetherness to remain there on higher and higher levels. But without this awareness and without allowing, training of horse and rider may achieve a high level in terms of exercises, but it will remain mechanical. True mastery, the true harmony, comes out of togetherness, which comes from a state of non-doing. Of simply allowing your body and your horse to move as one, directed from your intent, with your previously learned techniques as a background program to steer things in the right direction.

Survival Responses

On my 32nd birthday my former husband, a lifelong fanatic in skiing and snowboarding, took me on a winter holiday. He thought it would be fun if I learned how to snowboard. I'd never been on a winter holiday before because I was afraid of getting hurt. To be injured and unable to work is a terrible thought for a self-employed horse trainer, so getting on a board on a slippery slope and risking my body and my livelihood was a big step. After a few hours of snowboard lessons I understood the basic techniques and the topic 'turns' came up. But no matter how much I willed myself to position my snowboard vertically on the slope and no matter how well I understood the technical aspects, each time I started to turn my board and gathered speed, my body froze and I fell. A survival part of my brain took over and made my breathing shallow and my muscles stiffen. Practicing on the baby slope, I simply could not will my body into doing what I was taught to do. This is fear at its most basic level. The fear of hurting yourself. Your brain realizes that whatever you have decided to do, it is not natural and we simply are not made to accelerate on a board down a slippery slope. We don't want to get hurt. The brain takes over, freezes the body, and in the end, because you freeze, you fall. A little voice inside you goes: "See? You shouldn't be here on this board in the first place!"

To learn to overrule this survival instinct, to respond in a completely opposite way and change my habits was probably one of the most confrontational things I experienced in a long time. It made me realize how fearful some beginning (and some not-so beginner) riders must feel. Since I have been riding, jumping and doing crazy things on horseback ever since I was a little child, I have never experienced this level of basic fear around horses. A training horse that gets a bit too enthusiastic in the canter and throws in some bucks is met with a loud "Yihaa" and a big smile. Because I know how to position my body and my horse's body to keep things safe for both of us. Because I have been in similar situations before and got out of them unharmed. Because I know what to do next. I can continue to breathe and remain calm. It was not the same on the board, because I had not experienced a positive outcome often enough to 'program' the proper responses in my body and brain.

Learning how to snowboard made me aware of how frustrating a yell of "just do it!" can be from someone who is comfortable, experienced and not afraid. I realized that it takes a lot of practice in a safe environment to build up enough confidence. I learned how practicing too much or how being tired or getting another negative experience (a particularly painful fall) can ruin all the trust and confidence you had built up before. How too much thinking and analyzing gets in the way of simply being and doing and how, in the end, things start to get better when you manage to clear your mind, breathe and visualize a successful outcome.

No matter how well we understand what to do on a cognitive level, why to do it and how to do it, our brain can get in the way of allowing the right thing to happen. The primitive part of our brain can overrule our rational thoughts. When your mind blocks your body, all the technique you've learned simply can't help you. Your body cannot do what the rational part of your brain wants you to do when habits, beliefs or fear get in the way. Your body and mind can't be separated; they are one. Under stress your survival-brain makes your body act and react. This is not always functional when we practice sports such as snowboarding or horseback riding, given that these sports demand some counter-intuitive responses. For example, to keep on breathing and not tense up when your horse spooks. Or to give on the reins, bend your horse and use your inside leg instead of pulling on both reins when you feel your horse gets too fast.

The good news is that you can learn to overcome this basic fear response. By building up positive experiences and by practicing the same basic forms and movements over and over again. With training, you can shape your habits and patterns. After one year of practice, my initial reflex of stiffening up when my snowboard accelerated had changed to the reflex of bending my knees and shifting my weight. I had learned how to control the speed of the board with my body and now can play with the turns. I will never be a fantastic snowboard as that requires more practice, but I have learned the basic techniques needed to come down a slope safely – with a smile on my face.

Always Back to Basics!

In one riding lesson or another, many students may have sighed to themselves, "Oh, basic work, again!" But yes, the work of educating ourselves and our horses is always about refining the basics. In this basic work, which for me consists of circles, lateral movements and transitions, I increasingly refine my posture, breathing, awareness and movement. And then, when I continue onto the more schooled exercises, I test if I can bring this refinement into collection.

In the martial arts, it is very normal to study the same exercises throughout the entire course of training. Masters and beginners study the same movements, although they may look completely different. In Japanese, these detailed choreographed patterns of movements are called *kata*. By practicing repetitively the student develops the ability to execute the techniques and movements naturally, without thinking or analyzing. The student practices internalizing the movements and techniques of kata so they can be executed without thought or hesitation. A beginner's movements will look uneven and difficult while a master's will appear simple and flowing. Not all forms are that complicated but there are layers to them. In the beginning, you have to remember the sequence and the movements. At a certain point, you know them and can focus on how smoothly one movement flows into the next. These can be practiced and perfected throughout your entire life!

Horse riding is no different. By practicing the same circles, lateral movements and transitions again and again, both horse and rider will acquire a more natural, flowing quality in the movements. The movements become reflex-like and soft. The better educated the horse and rider are, the more subtle, nuanced and refined the rider's aids become. And this quality can be taken up to higher and higher levels. But the foundation remains the quality of the basic work. The more fluent that is, the better the advanced movements will be. So, practicing the basics again and again is never a waste of time. It is not even boring because you can discover new layers every time when you try to perfect your movements.

So, instead of thinking that you should really be practicing flying changes by now, appreciate all the time you spend on the basic work because this is where the real quality is found and refined.

Empty Shells

Often, the instructions from a riding teacher end up being executed to the point where things get overdone, resulting in a caricature. Or the students follows the instructions using different muscles and body parts than the instructor intended, resulting in a lookalike. A teacher tries to transmit an experience to the students and is using words to describe these feelings and experiences. The student translates these words into a certain action. As the student is not the riding teacher, the words may mean something else for the student then they do for the riding teacher. A different experience or no experience at all is linked to these words. This often leads to confusion or misunderstanding. An honest student would tell the instructor, "These instructions mean nothing to me." But most students are too polite or shy to admit this. They just try to do their best without knowing what exactly they are looking for. Words are like empty shells that we must fill with empirical feelings. We need to experience the meaning of these words and instructions before the words have any importance to us.

When the student (by accident or with the help from the teacher) has had the same experience as the teacher, then later on the instructions can be used to remind the student of that previous experience, to re-find the same feeling the student had before. Then, the student can get that feeling back and the instructions will have the right effect. The rider and instructor speak the same language. Both have filled the same shells with the same meaning. But when a student has not had the exact same experience the teacher has had, and has linked some other body use or some other feeling to the instructions, then things get more difficult. Simply following instructions without knowing what experience you are looking for often doesn't give you the same results.

An example: I was teaching a beginner rider on one of my school horses. She had been riding the same horse more often and we had built up the understanding and use of her seat, movement and awareness to the point where she was ready to have her first experience of collection. As she was a smart, analytical and theoretical person, I started by explaining the goal of the exercises and the theory behind half halts. Then, we

put things into practice with me talking her through the collection and extensions. Step by step I explained what her body should do. She managed to follow my instructions to the letter, but things remained a bit stiff and mechanical. That was quite normal, because she needed the analytical part of her brain to translate my instructions into actions in her own body. Then, with her in the saddle, I took my school horse in hand and asked him to collect and her to simply sit, relax and feel. Then it really clicked. She felt what we were looking in her body. Afterwards, she managed to collect the horse by herself, just by re-finding the same experience in her body.

It is as if your brain contains a web of information. A connection of concepts and experiences. A network of shells, both empty and full ones. When a new idea or exercise is very closely linked to what already exists in that web, you can easily add this new thing. This is why in both horses and humans, when we teachers build up our lessons and exercises in the right step-by-step way, both horse and riding student can easily follow the new concepts and continue to develop. They add full shells to their network. When a new concept or experience is still far from anything the horse or human has learned and experienced before, they have nowhere in their brain to link this new information to. The shell may be added to the network, but is still empty, waiting for the right experience to fill it. Before it can start to have meaning, you need to have had some similar idea or experience before. I get this when I read books. Each time I open a book by an old master and read the text that, for example, Steinbrecht, Pluvinel or Guerinière wrote so many years ago, I ask myself "Was this in here before?" Each time I open that book, something new stands out. Of course, it was already there. Only when I read it before I couldn't match the information to any of my own experiences. The moment that I am working on that topic, I suddenly see and grasp the concept of their words. I can fill another shell.

If you have had a certain experience or feeling, often just thinking about that experience or feeling already creates changes in your body. It changes your muscle tone and balance, without you doing anything. Then the idea is that you simply allow your body and your horse to move. Start to do, to act consciously, and things become mechanical.

Start to allow, and things will flow. But before you can allow something to happen, you need to have an idea of what it is that you want to happen. You need to have had the experience before. So simply getting on your horse, doing nothing and wishing for some experience to come to you may not be the solution. In the beginning, you have to do things, experiment, try things out. Do too much. Read. Watch videos. Then, by accident or on purpose, the right experience, the right feeling may happen when you ride. The next time, you can do less and allow for more of the same thing to happen. From then on, as things get easier for you and your horse, you can do less and less, and you can start to think only of what you want and let it happen. That is where the 'Less is More' quote from Centered Riding® really works. You can do less of something when you have the right thing to do less of. But before you can do less, sometimes you have to do more of something to find the right something.

Now Is the Moment!

It may seem obvious to you, but you can only ride NOW. That is: in the present moment. *"You cannot ride yesterday and you cannot ride tomorrow,"* Bent Branderup, Grandmaster of the Academic Art of Riding, always says. He sees a lot of riders who try to ride the way they would like to ride in the future; over-asking their horses with exercises that are still too complicated for the rider, the horse or both. Instead, they need to be aware of what they can ask of their horses in this moment, and of what they are capable of themselves, slowly building communication, coordination and muscles. You can ride only with what you've got. That means that you can only ask to do exercises on the level that the weakest link (rider or horse) can execute with ease. From that level, things can develop step by step, bringing horse-and-rider combinations to a higher and higher level over time.

My teacher, Tom Nagel, asks this question when he is teaching his Rider's Seat clinics: *"Can there be thoughts in the present moment?"* It often leads to confusion among the participants. First of all, what does a question about thoughts in the present moment have to do with horse riding? Then people start to ponder the question until Tom helps them find the answer to this Zen riddle: All thoughts are in the present moment, you can only think NOW. Every thought is born in the present moment. However, no thought is ABOUT the present moment. While you formulate your thought, the present moment has already passed… Follow me one step further: if thoughts are never about the present moment, then they must always be about something in the past, or about something yet to come. And that is exactly what thoughts are!

Back to riding: Riding with thoughts about what happened before or what you want to happen in the future takes you away from what is going on right NOW. Of course, after your ride or after an exercise, you can take time to look back on what happened, what went well and how you want to change things for the next time. This is sensible and is called reflection, which is a very important part of learning. Also, you are allowed to think ahead, as you must have some kind of a plan for when and where you will make your next transition. This is also sensible and is called 'clear intent' in Centered Riding®. However,

you need to limit yourself to these very practical, short thoughts that are appropriate for your riding in this present moment. Thinking about your upcoming competition, feeling disappointed or extremely proud about your last trot-halt transition half a long-side ago, or fantasizing about what wonderful things you and your horse may do in the future is taking you out of the present moment. And the present moment is exactly where your horse is, always. The less you are in the now, the less you can be there for your horse and connect with him. The more you think over what just happened or what you would like in future, the less your body and mind are receptive to what is going on right now. Your horse will feel it, respond to it and may seem less focused or disconnected. And, you may not register some of the great things your horse is offering you!

The best way for me to get into the now is to apply Zen meditation methods to my riding. An awareness on my breathing and posture quietens down all unnecessary thoughts and brings me into the NOW. My breathing and posture are always in the present moment. I cannot use the breath I took a minute ago, and I cannot ride with a posture that I may or may not have in the future. So being aware of my current breath and posture always brings me into the now.

You can start with this awareness before you go and make contact with your horse. Take a few breaths to clear your head. After you have mounted and started your warm up walk, take this time to check your body alignment, your movement and your breathing. Then take this with you into your ride. Observe rather than judge. Things will be more in flow, your senses will heighten and your riding will improve. Leave each step that has been made behind you, don't look back. Ride every stride as it comes, with your awareness on your body and the body of the horse and your minds connected. Don't anticipate what may or may not happen, take everything as it comes, without judgment. It doesn't matter if that exercise was good or bad, it is already in the past. Take what you need to learn from it and carry on. Don't let judgment or anticipation get in the way. Your responsibility is to keep up with your horse, and he is in the now every step of his way. So don't linger in the past and don't get ahead of yourself thinking about the future. Be in the now, so you can meet your horse where he is and you can move together from there.

Imagine...

Have you ever considered the power of your imagination? Visualizing what you want has such an impact that your brain will send impulses to your muscles and change your tissue and movement.

A very easy way to prove this is the following exercise I learned from a Feldenkrais practitioner, which is also used in Centered Riding®:

Stand up straight, with your feet at hip width and your knees and ankles unlocked. Stretch your right arm straight in front of you to shoulder height. Then, slowly, move your arm at shoulder height to your right and as far back as you can. Follow with your body but do not move your feet. How far can you turn around? Look over your outstretched arm and remember the place in the room your hand is pointing toward. Then, slowly, turn back and when the arm is straight in front of you again, drop the arm down to your side.

Now, lift the same arm again. This time, keep your body still and move only the arm to the right, and then back to the front, but at the same time also turn your head to your LEFT. Repeat this three times and take a moment to relax the arm. Then, when your arm is back at the front, turn your arm and your head to the right, but this time roll your EYES to the left. Repeat three times and relax. Then bring the arm up and turn your entire body again following the arm to the right like you did the first time and check: where is your hand pointing now? Did you get further than the first time?

Now, do the same with your left arm and see where you are pointing toward. When you are facing front again, drop the arm. This time, go through the entire sequence again, only with the left arm. But you will not DO it, you will IMAGINE that you are doing it. So in reality, you leave the arm hanging relaxed at your side, but in your mind you lift your left arm and bring it three times to the left and back to the center while at the same time you imagine your head to the right. Then, imagine both arm and head turning to the left but your eyes rolling to the right, three times. Then open your eyes. Turn your arm and body to the left.

And? Did you get further round with the left arm as well? That is the power of your imagination.

Just thinking about a certain movement makes your brain send signals to the muscles involved, activating them. By separating your arm, head and neck and even your eyes, the whole chain gets a bit more activated, resulting in a bigger turn when you put all parts together again. No matter whether you have moved your body parts separately or only imagined moving them, when you move them together again afterwards the movement gets more efficient. The cool thing is that we do not necessarily need to actually move. Just thinking about it gives a response in our brain and body! The more often you have executed these movements before, the bigger the power of your imagination is. Because when you have done it before, your brain and body remember how it 'should be'. So you can imagine a beautiful piaffe in your body, but unless you have actually experienced how it feels to be on a school master in a perfect piaffe, the imagination will fall short somewhere.

This is how we can also train body parts that are a bit more stiff or unwilling on the horse. Do you have a stiffer leg? Or one that tends to pull up? Simply go home, lie on your back with your legs bent, close your eyes and imagine the movement of your hips, knees and ankles while you ride. Imagine both legs making a soft, perfect up-and-down movement. There is no 'bad' leg. They both move fantastically in your head. Repeat these visualizations frequently, and you will start to have two superb legs when you are on your horse too!

What Do You Fear?

Everyone has fears. It is a normal survival thing. If your ancestors had had no fear, they would have walked right into that bear or into the lion's den and they would not have survived to reproduce. You would not have existed without some basic fear in your ancestors which helped them to stay alive. Fear motivates us to undertake action. This can be fight or flight. Fear heightens our senses, it makes us alert and ready for action.

We may not live in the wild anymore and many of our instincts may have diminished, but fear has never left us. What has happened is that we have shifted the cause of our fear: from physical threats to our emotional state. That's right: most things that we are afraid of nowadays are in our head. These fear-causing thoughts are very poisonous. As with all of our thoughts: what you give attention grows. So the more you focus on your fears, the bigger they become. Many people live with the continuous presence of emotional fear. Thoughts of being not good enough, insecurities about our body or our performance, the fear of not being seen and heard, fear of losing our loved ones, fear of being alone, just to name a few. This causes our body to be in an unnecessary state of stress and readiness and that drains our energy. In the wild, once in safety from that bear or lion, our adrenaline levels would go down again and our bodies could return to their normal peaceful state. But with a constant flow of negative or fearful thoughts, our bodies are in a heightened stress level all the time. That is unhealthy and tiring. That is what can cause burnout or depression.

Our thoughts are funny things: the more you think of something, the more real it becomes. The more attention you give to your pain, the more your pain will try to define you. The more attention you give to your fears, the more the fear will try to define you. But you can't just push these feelings and thoughts away either. A good start is to decide not to let your fear define you. You are not your fear.

I encounter many riders with fear. The most essential one being the fear of falling and hurting oneself. This fear is quite close to the fear our ancestors must have experienced in the wild: if you fall, you can hurt yourself. You could die and leave your children as orphans. This

is a physical fear. It makes your body tense, your breathing shallow and your adrenaline goes up. Most horses react to this physical fear response by following their leader: if you get afraid, so do they. The chance that you will fall off and hurt yourself goes up exponentially. The more positive experiences you have in riding, by not falling off the horse, and the more experience you get in your seat and your aids, the smaller the chance will be that you will actually fall and get injured. And with growing confidence comes a different attitude that the horse will respond to.

Besides this basic physical fear, there are emotional fears in horse riding too. "My horse doesn't like me" or "I'm not sure if I am good enough to give my horse what he needs" are classic thoughts. The fear of rejection, the fear of not being good enough. These fears often make you unsure, hesitant, doubting yourself and others. They lead to the same physical manifestations and the same stress-response in yourself and your horse as a physical fear would do. These fears are much harder to work with. Because the only one who can give you positive experiences and make you change your thoughts is you. How? Start by recognizing your thoughts. Identify your fear. Think: "Ah, there I go again with my thought of not being good enough." Try to find out where it comes from. When you were a child did an adult tell you that you were not good enough? Is there a certain event you can remember where your emotional fear started?

Ask yourself: is this thought and this fear useful in this situation? If your answer is no, make some resolutions that are opposite to what you fear. If you are afraid your horse does not like you, make a new plan: "I am going to like my horse." Do things you both enjoy and see the enjoyment in your horse's eye. Horses are the perfect mirror. If you are afraid they don't like you, they will react to your self-doubt with distance and hesitation or a total lack of respect. And that will confirm your fearful thoughts. If you can change that, and take control over your thoughts by changing them into a positive, you will see your horse respond in a positive way.

Don't see fear as something annoying, but embrace it as something that can teach you about yourself and that can give you tools for self-improvement. If you can identify and change your fearful thoughts, you can do anything you want!

THE RIDER'S BODY

Who Needs Fixing?

The moment one starts to ride the focus can be neither completely on the movement and posture of the horse nor only on the posture of the rider. Riding is a dialogue between rider and horse. The rider does something, the horse feels it, responds to it and the rider reflects on the horse's answer and corrects by giving a new signal where necessary. My experience is that most of the time the rider is the limiting factor. The horse knows how to balance himself and was taught so even more from the ground work training we do in the Academic Art of Riding. He understands the aids we taught him from the ground and knows where to place his feet. We humans have invested time and money in manual therapy for our horses, lessons and training in ground work, quality tack and so on. But we forget to work on ourselves. Then, with our stiff, unbalanced bodies and bad posture, we climb on our wonderfully balanced and prepared horses and wonder why they lose balance, fall on the shoulders and drop their backs. Often, we then start to 'correct' our horses by using more of our secondary aids of legs and reins. But the truth is: When you get on your horse's back; don't start by 'fixing' your horse. Start by fixing yourself.

Try to go on a hike with a heavy, unbalanced backpack on your back. One side is heavier than the other. You feel a constant pull to that more loaded side and it will be hard to walk perfectly straight. Then imagine running with it and besides the backpack not being straight, it also starts to bounce against your back. Does that make you want to go out the next day and repeat the same thing? Of course not. Instead, you will probably try to redistribute the weight in your backpack to make it more comfortable to carry. Luckily for us, we can adjust our backpacks. Unluckily for our horses, they just have to make do with whatever weight they get on their back. Horses can't choose their rider, so we should at least make their job as comfortable as possible. By balancing and straightening our bodies, we can give clearer aids to our horses and not disturb them as much.

Because we often speak about horse training, we often find ourselves believing in the misconception that it is the horse that needs most of the

work, most of the 'fixing'. While in fact it is us, the riders, who have to strive constantly for self-improvement mentally and physically in order to allow the horse to move correctly. A horse without a rider is still a horse. What is a rider without a horse? Only human. We need to make the bigger step in our development to match our horses. All good rider train, both on and off the horse, to improve their own mental and physical state. It is the training off the horse that allows you to focus 100% on yourself. And actually, while training on your horse, keep 90% of your focus on you and only 10% on your horse. Ask yourself: "What can I do, in my body, in my attitude and in the way that I ask my horse to do something that will make it easier for him to understand and execute the movements?"

When Crooked Feels Straight...

"When crooked feels straight, straight feels crooked," I often tell my students. My teachers have often told me the same. And it is truly so. As a bodywork practitioner, I work with re-aligning riders on my table. When I start with a new client I ask them to lie on their back and position themselves 'straight' on the table. Most times, when they claim to be straight, I have to re-adjust their head, pelvis and legs to align them. When I ask them how they feel once I have positioned them straight on the table, they always say: "Crooked." What you are used to is your truth. When you are used to being crooked, your body will feel straight to you. Your brain will tell you something is off when you truly align yourself. Until body and brain get used to the new straight. Bodywork helps to integrate body and mind and find alignment. But it takes time before you find your own 'straight'. And it takes time for the horse to find his 'straight' too. With your help, he may find it. But only when you have found your own.

Our brains are tricky that way. They can fool us, making us think that we are straight, or moving, while in fact we are not. Most of us have been in a situation where you think you are doing something else than you are actually doing. When you look at yourself in the mirror or look back on yourself in a video it looks completely different than what you thought you were doing. Our inner picture of ourselves and the picture on the outside do not match.

An example: in one of my seat clinics I was recently teaching, one of the women participating was a Centered Riding® instructor. I had introduced the concept of the spiraling spine to the group, a concept which was already familiar to her. When she got on her horse for her lesson we worked on one of my classic exercises: spiraling in, making the circle smaller, and while continuing the inward spiral in the spine and maintaining the bending in the horse, move the horse with your inside leg into a bigger circle again. This exercise is great for the riders to practice the spiral of their spine and the correct movement of hips and legs. It also works wonders for the suppleness and roundness of the horse (See: The Spiraling Spine).

This woman, familiar with the concept of both the movement of the hips and the spiral of the spine, was barely moving at all. The result was a horse that was stiff most of the time, straight and going against the hand. In her mind though, she was moving as much as she needed to be. When I asked her to over-do the exercise she proclaimed, surprised: "Even MORE than what I am already doing?" When she finally started to allow her spine to really spiral and her upper legs to really lift and drop from the hip joints, to her it felt like she was moving way too much. But finally, her horse started to bend, relax and step under. Afterwards, she told me that she had believed that 'less is more.' And that is quite often true, it just needs to be the right 'less.' Not moving is not doing less, it is being stiff. This is an example of how our inner picture and outer picture can differ.

The next clinic, the rider was there again, allowing her body to be moved much more compared to the first time and she was exactly in the movement with her horse. Her horse had suppled up. Because they were moving together it looked as if she was hardly moving at all during the exercises. Although it still felt to her that she was moving a lot, she recognized the difference and keeps working on it.

Our bodies often do something different than we think they do. Simply because we are used to a certain feeling. This has become our 'normal.' Anything in a different alignment feels out of balance. When you have always sat slightly slumped, sitting upright may give you the feeling of leaning back. When you have always carried your spine with a hollow lower back, sitting vertically may feel like being hunched forward. Anything with more movement then you are used to may feel huge. Anything with a different movement may feel wrong. That is why when we ride, mirrors can be an important tool to see what you are doing. Without mirrors, video yourself when you ride so you can look back on yourself later on, and see if what you felt and what you see match. Are your inner picture and outer picture the same? A pair of expert eyes on the ground to give you feedback and suggestions is something even the best riders need to correct themselves once in a while. And, of course, to listen to your horse. If you are not sure about a certain posture or movement, check how your horse is moving. Is his back free, swinging and round or does he get stiffer? The movement of your horse will tell you if what you are doing is right.

Healthy Body, Healthy Mind

Your body use affects your brain; it affects your mood, your feelings, and your beliefs. If you have poor posture you will be more inclined to be depressed and tired. When you are in pain it will be hard to stay cheerful. The same goes for our horses. When your horse has poor posture, a sore back or sore feet, his energy, self-confidence and liveliness will be poor and his place in the hierarchy in the herd he lives in will be low. With correct posture and good balance, your horse will have a different attitude in the herd. I see many rehabilitation horses rise in the hierarchy of our herd when they start to feel better in their bodies. One of my personal goals – and a goal in the Academic Art of Riding – is to train horses in a way that they start to feel proud and beautiful. And this is what we riders should feel too! When you yourself are fit, carry yourself upright and with energy, you will radiate that energy outwards. You will change the world around you and you will change yourself and your riding.

By working on your body you will change how you feel about yourself. The quickest way to change is through the body. A healthy body brings about a healthy mind. And because your feeling about yourself changes you will send out a different energy. The people and horses around you will pick this up. They say horses are your mirror, but in fact all living beings around you are. It is just that animals respond more directly to what they sense than most people. If you start to actively work on your posture, you will be amazed by how quickly you will also notice a change in how you feel. No matter how poor or how good your posture is to begin with, we can all change for the better. And with this better posture we can all start to feel better too and have deeper experiences with ourselves and the people and animals around us.

The key to a happy life and a happy horse? Find a way to work on your posture each day. OUTSIDE of your riding time. There are many ways you can do this: You can sit on the ground on a meditation cushion with your legs folded or sit on a stool with a hard, straight seat with both feet flat on the floor and practice actively supporting yourself upright. When you sit, always have your hips higher than your knees. You can

also take one of the many tai chi stances, for example the (appropriately called) horse stance. Whatever you choose, take a moment each day to repeat this position and watch your posture: is your tail bone hanging down, is your spine vertical and are your chin and forehead in the same vertical plane? How long can you stay in this position without tensing up? Can you continue to breathe relaxed and deep?

Not big on standing or sitting still? Then go for a long walk in nature each day, being mindful of the way you carry yourself, how you place your feet and how you breathe. Is your head moving while you walk? Observe yourself while you muck out your horse boxes or sweep your yard. Become aware of your posture and movements in each activity during the day.

No matter if it is two minutes or 30 minutes that you can keep this up: start with what you are comfortable with and then make this time period a bit longer each day. In doing so you will be actively improving your posture and you will train your mind to come into a relaxed focus. By making the time a bit longer each day, you are expanding your comfort zone. It is amazing how much energy a few minutes of being observant like this each day can give you. Then, when you ride your horse, remember this posture you have when you sit or stand and bring the same posture into your riding. This way you add extra posture training time to your day. Also, watch your posture when you sit behind the computer, at the dining table, while driving your car. You have so many hours in the day in which you can practice! And the more upright, proud and beautiful your posture becomes, the more energy, vitality and happiness you will experience and give to those around you.

Defining 'the Seat'

The seat is an important instrument in all disciplines and levels of riding. We use our body to physically connect with the horse whenever we ride. We use our body to transfer our requests for the horse into aids. Our body is the tool of the horse-riding artist. It is widely known that a good rider relies on the seat as the main aid for the horse. The ideal is to give signals to the horse that are so small that they are almost unnoticeable for spectators, that use the slightest movement in the rider's seat, directed only by clear intent. The leg and rein aids become mere extensions of the rider's body.

This is why I find it so important, in the first level of the Art of Riding, to first understand and teach the basic aspects of the seat before teaching people secondary aids such as legs and reins. We need to understand how the seat of a rider can be a communication tool and can support the training of the horse. We also need to understand how the seat of the rider develops as the horse develops during its lifelong training. We need to discover how our bodies work, which movement patterns and habits we have in our body that are dysfunctional in riding and which movement patterns and habits we need in order to improve our communication with our horses.

Defining the seat is already the first difficult part. What do we mean when we talk about the seat? Some people define it as the rider's pelvis, hip joints and seat bones. Others say the seat is the part that wraps around the horse's back: the pelvis plus the upper legs of the rider (from knee to knee). As we use our entire body to ride our horses, the seat is in fact the entire body. Maybe we should not use the word 'seat' at all, as it may make people think about just their sitting part. Maybe the proper term would simply be 'the rider's body' instead of 'the rider's seat'.

So, then, what is a good seat, or a good body use of the rider?

A good rider:

- moves all body parts in rhythm with the movement of the horse
- allows the horse to move by being supple and moveable in all joints
- balances to allow the horse to find his balance
- is sending energy forward through the reins and never pulls
- rides with the maximum length (vertical alignment) of the spine and allows the horse to do the same (horizontal alignment)
- can position the body in the shape the horse should move in
- uses the inner core, the psoas muscles, for balance, stability and flexibility and relaxes the outer muscles such as the abdominals
- can use all body parts (hands, legs, etc.) independently from each other
- uses the breath as a way to rebalance both rider and horse
- matches the body to the needs, balance and training level of the horse

Once the rider has found the correct posture, movement and correct breathing, it is possible to stay 'out of the horse's way' and allow the horse to move in balance. Of course, then comes the time when the rider has to progress from merely being transported to actually communicate with the horse through body use.

The more someone has already trained with body awareness methods such as Alexander Technique, yoga or has practiced martial arts, the better aligned and balanced the rider is. As my Centered Riding® teacher, Karen Irland says: "The more you develop yourself off the horse, the more you develop on the horse." And let's be fair to our horses too: as long as you cannot manage moving your own body in balance, why bother the horse with it? Better work on yourself on the ground first, and then bring your well aligned and balanced body to your horse.

The Development of the Seat throughout History

The seat must be functional rather than pretty. This is clearly demonstrated when we look at it from a historical perspective. We should start by making a distinction between the northwestern European history of riding, which was used for close combat warfare on horseback, and cultures where horses were used in long-distance warfare, using bow and arrow or other long-distance weapons. For these latter riders, the challenge was to balance on a high-speed horse on rough terrain.

The Eurasian warriors perfected the skill of long-distance riding on horseback so that they could use both hands to wield their weapons. We still find examples of this mastery of balance in cultures such as Mongolia where the proud descendants of Genghis Khan still ride in their traditional way. Most Mongolians in the countryside still have a semi-nomadic existence and learn to ride before they can walk. On my visits to this country I was often amazed by their flexibility of their seat. On 100 kilometer trips these people stand in their short stirrups, sit on the front pommel of their saddle, on the back cantle, and hang on the left side of their horse and on the right side of their horse. They constantly move around and are not concerned about whether it 'looks pretty' or not. As long as they move comfortably from A to B and have their hands free to wield a lasso, shotgun, carry their birds, or play on their mobile phones, they are fine.

I spent many kilometers on my Mongolian horse cantering side by side with my Mongolian guide while bent over a Mongolian phrasebook. Showing my guide a sentence, listening to his pronunciation, repeating after him and practicing the next one. My horse maintained his steady canter over the huge steppes for many kilometers. The horizon hardly changed. Me, shifting my weight around constantly as the short stirrups prevent you from sitting down and force you to be flexible in your hips, knees and ankle joints. Mongolian multi-tasking at its best, but not the friendliest to the horse's back. I remember that when I got back home after five months the people around me commented on how my seat had changed. I was way more stable yet flexible on my own horse at home

and less impressed by any sudden jolts or bucks. Unfortunately I had also developed a very relaxed slump in my upper body that took me quite a while to correct again afterwards.

For the mainland northwestern European riders, close combat on horseback made it necessary to find a seat in which they could brace themselves against the impact of their weapons. In the Renaissance, saddles had a high cantle behind to prevent the rider from falling backward off their horse on impact. These riders used long stirrups and stretched their legs out while pressing their heels down. This gave them the brace they needed to stay on while impacting with their weapons.

In Western Europe, when war techniques changed and close combat on horses was no longer practiced, the nobility started equitation 'pour plaisir' (for fun). Showing horses, parading them around became their spare time activity. In these days of the Baroque, the riders no longer needed this brace. They started to balance on their seat bones and let their legs hang naturally.

For these riders, educating the horse was still based on the 'classical' movements used in battle to impress the enemy, to defend oneself or attack the enemy. In the High School jumps, horses were supposed to land on their hind legs. This had various functions: the horse's raised neck protected the rider from the front and it made the landing more comfortable as the impact of landing was absorbed by the horse bending his joints in the hind quarter. When different riding cultures started to mix and riding officers were required to ride both forward from A to B and still be able to collect their horses and make small jumps, these ideas from the mainland were still very much present. Riders were seated much more upright going over a fence. This changed in the early 19th century with the Italian rider Caprilli. Since then, people have shortened their stirrups and gone more forward with the movement of the horse when they jump.

Nowadays the notion is that the rider should balance his body parts vertically with an imaginary line through ear, shoulder, hip and heel. This is correct on a horizontally balanced horse. On a horse that is not

moving in this horizontal equilibrium a rider may have to alter her alignment to be slightly more diagonally forward (with, in the extreme case, the racing seat you see in jockeys) or slightly diagonally backward in a collected seat (with, in the extreme case, the leaning back you see in riders in the levade). In a vertical alignment on a horizontally balanced horse you can ride more forward into extension, jump and collect by changing the angle of your spine. The 'basic' seat that puts both rider and horse in neutral is with the vertical alignment of the rider and the horizontal balance of the horse.

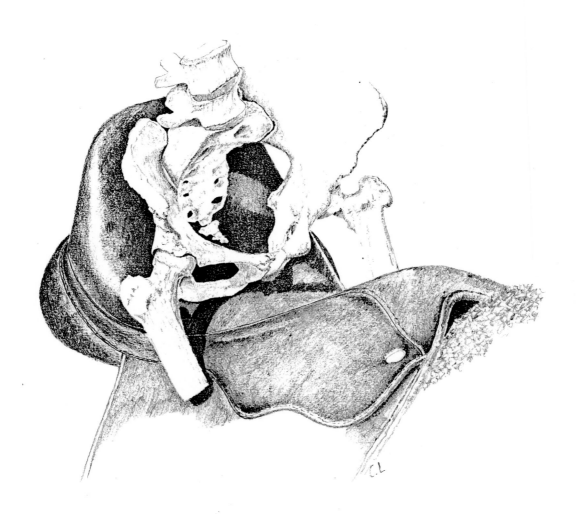

Four Cornerstones in Riding

I learned from Tom Nagel that horseback riding consists of the three training elements of Zazen (literally 'seated meditation'): posture, breathing and awareness. While sitting Zazen we train to maintain our correct, stable and relaxed posture with our breathing. While sitting Zazen we keep a 180 degree awareness with our eyes and a 360 degree awareness with our other senses. We are training to be aware of the space around us and the energy in this space. When we practice these elements in sitting, martial arts or horseback riding, we can enter the state of mind called Samadhi. When we sit Zazen we sit still. While practicing martial arts or horseback riding we need to find these elements while moving and physically interacting with another living being. For riding, the fourth very important element is movement.

Let's explore these four elements a bit closer:

Posture: A good posture means having all parts of the body balanced on top of each other, using the skeleton to carry most of the weight. When the posture is correct, you use your core (psoas) muscles (See 'The Pelvis and the True Core') – the primary connectors between your torso and your legs that affect your posture – to stabilize your spine. These muscles are toned, while the muscles more to the outside of the body stay soft and relaxed. In the traditional riding instructions, this is described as the line from ear, shoulder, hip and heel. That is correct, but we need to discover how to place our body parts in that alignment without tensing and stiffening. It means using our skeleton to 'stack up' all our body parts and let the weight be carried by the bones. We use only the muscles we need on the inside to stabilize our skeleton. The psoas muscles play an important part in stabilizing the lower back and pelvis and placing the legs in the correct position.

Breathing: Good breathing supports your posture. In other words, with good vertical breathing you maintain your alignment easily and without tension. Also, your exhalations will allow you to relax all the muscles you may have tensed. (See 'Breathing Up and Down')

Awareness: The result of training your posture and breathing is a different sense of awareness. Awareness of yourself, your horse and your surroundings. In Alexander Technique, they teach you to think about the space behind you and to maintain a panoramic vision. This allows you to 'fill out' our back and find your vertical alignment. In Zazen, we speak of looking 180 degree with the eyes and 360 degree awareness.

Movement: Breathing brings movement. A correct posture brings movement. Awareness brings movement. On a horse, we move all the time. But even sitting Zazen or standing in the 'rider stance' in tai chi for minutes on end without moving, we are moving. Our breath is moving us all the time. Our inner processes, circulation and metabolism is moving. Our awareness is bringing movement and the flow of energy to various parts of our body and connecting that flow to the outside world. We are constantly refining our posture, finding alignment and relaxing our body parts. Even when we are completely still. When we stop moving, we are dead.

On a moving horse, our movements are always three dimensional: we are being moved up and down, forward and back and to the left and right, because our horses have a three-dimensional swing in their spine. The ribcage of the horse on which our upper legs lie, is moving with each stride. This brings movement into our legs and hip joints. Also, our pelvis is moved, as our seat bones rest on the horse's back, on each side of his spine.

It is important to give movement a direction. The main direction through our body is up or vertical. The main direction from our arms is forward. We should never stop any movement anywhere, but it is important to channel the direction clearly for the horse into a 'forward and up' direction.

Seat Training?

Have you ever had seat lessons? Lessons of the kind where it doesn't matter how your horse is moving, you just focus on yourself? During a lesson it can be very educational for a rider to focus once or twice only on her own body use and movements and not actively 'shape' the horse. In such a lesson you don't use your body to communicate with your horse while you ride but just practice your own movements. In that moment you are not actually riding, you are just being transported. That's OK, too. It's just different thing from actual riding and should be a conscious choice.

When you do this with a school master horse that knows how to carry himself or that is being shaped by someone from the ground, it's very pleasant to do. It lets you experience how a horse should actually move and how your body should move with it. But if you do this kind of seat training on a horse that has problems with his own balance and/or body, it is not fair on the horse. You cannot let the horse go round in a bad shape while you sit on his back doing whatever you like for yourself. To carry someone who is not an active part of the horse-and-rider combination and who may even work against the horse's movements, while trying to figure out her own body use makes it very hard work for the horse. It is as if you are giving all the responsibility for correct equilibrium to the horse. And making him figure it out. Most horses will suffer physically from this. The most damaged rehabilitation horse I ever had was a former therapeutic riding horse that had been carrying spastic people around who constantly threw themselves off balance. With her good nature this mare endured and patiently carried these riders for many years. Until she was physically completely damaged. She did great work in the therapeutic riding center and had many fans. She gave a lot. But her body paid the price in the end.

It is not a good idea to just focus on the 'perfect' seat for a rider with a horse that has not yet reached an advanced level of training. It can be harmful to the horse as the horse may not walk in balance. There should always be mutual communication and a shared equilibrium. Even though your seat maybe not be the prettiest, it needs to be functional

in assisting you to train the horse. To help your horse move better. Therefore, the seat of the rider may look different over time, because as the horse starts to develop, the rider may evolve more and more toward that beautiful seat we all strive for. It is easy to sit and look pretty on a good-moving horse. It is almost impossible to sit and look pretty on a bad-moving horse and it is a much bigger achievement to use your seat to make a bad-moving horse move prettily!

Comparable Parts

Have you ever heard of the term 'comparable parts'? It means that we can take a look at our horse's body and our own, and see the similarities. We have the same muscles and the same bones. So, in most cases this rule applies: what is good biomechanics for a human to function is the same for our horse.

So, then, what is the main difference between how a human uses her body and how a horse uses his? We got up on our hind legs and started to walk upright. Our horses remained on all four feet. This means that our spine has a vertical alignment whereas our horse's spine has a horizontal alignment. But the same rules of biomechanics still apply!

For a healthy use of the body we want our horses to step under with their hind legs. Their hind legs need to come forward under their point of weight. This makes their pelvis tilt, brings their tail down and their back up. For us, the same rule applies; when you stand or walk or do martial arts, you want your knees to come forward while at the same time you 'drop your tail' which brings your waistline back and flattens your lower back. We want to walk a collected walk. Look around you in a busy street or at an airport. Most people walk with 'pushing hind legs'; they push their bodies forward by pushing their legs backward. This makes them move with their heads stuck out in front and a hollow lower back. They 'fall' forward into the movement and each stride has a moment of unbalance. Which is precisely how we do NOT want our horses to move!

If you want to help your horse move correctly, you have to sit properly on your horse. But it goes further than that. You help your horse the most by changing how you use your body in your entire daily life. Horses mirror us and we mirror our horses. Even from the ground. Even when we take them out of the field or brush them in the barn. Just like we subconsciously copy the posture of our parents, our teachers and our riding instructors. You are the biggest change when you can change yourself. It will influence the people and the horses around you when

you carry yourself with poise. Your upright posture will give you more energy and more confidence.

Also, when you ride, your horse will notice the difference. Sitting on his back with a hollowed back, your hips will be blocked and your upper legs will push the horse's back down, causing him to move with a dropped back himself. Flattening your lower back will free your hip joints and will enable the horse to move his spine and bring his back up. You want your horse to be 'rounded', to lengthen his upper line. By lengthening your own, you help your horse achieve this. In Alexander Technique they speak about letting your head go 'forward and up' while your tail drops down. You think your head away from your tail and your tail away from your head. This lengthens your own 'upper line'. We want our horses to do the same!

Your horse will pick up any tension in your body and he will respond to it. Some horses are more sensitive to tension than others but as your sensitivity and postural awareness develops, so does the sensitivity of your horse. We call it comparable parts because really, that is what it is. Your back and the horse's back are one in this horse-and-rider equilibrium. Your shoulders should move with his. Your legs should move with his hind legs. Your tension is his tension and your suppleness becomes the suppleness of the horse. In turns and side movements, this means that you will put your own body in the same position you want your horse's body to be positioned. Your head is placed parallel to your horse's head, your shoulders turn in the direction of the movement of your horse's front legs, and your legs follow the movement of your horse's hind legs. It also means that any tension in either you or your horse can be softened by moving your own body in that area of stiffness. Is your horse not releasing in his jaw? Move your own jaw gently. As Tom Nagel says: "Movement releases brace." Wherever you sense stiffness, gentle movements will not only loosen up yourself but also make your horse more supple. Put yourself in the shape and position you want your horse to move in and move in the way you would like your horse to move!

Being Centered, also from the Ground

Once we have established the basic relationship with the horse, we start their Academic training with work from the ground. In this Academic groundwork we teach our horses the aids and start with their physical training. We want our horses to gain suppleness, strength and to improve their balance. But we also carry our own postural and movement habits with us. Most of the time, we are not even aware of these habits. So I recommend working on your own body awareness and to practice useful and healthy habits right from the start! When we work on improving our horse's straightness, balance and coordination, we should also work on our own! Often, people seem to think that because we are not sitting on the horse in this stage, we will not be hindering him with our bodies. OK, we may not be adding any extra weight onto his back in groundwork, but we can definitely help or hinder our horse with the way we carry ourselves on the ground. This is why it is so important to consider your own posture and movement while working with your horse. Not only in riding, but also in groundwork, lunging, and in simply going out and meeting your horse in the field.

Horses communicate with body language. Out in the field in their herd, they may all seem to be 'just' grazing, but they can exchange around 250 signals per hour. Signals we mostly miss unless we pay specific attention. Horses are masters at responding to our body language too. Whether we use our body consciously or not, whatever message we send out with our posture, energy and movement, the horse will see it. They can read our posture, muscle tonus and our feelings. And, because they are used to responding to the expressions of other horses in their social group, they will also respond to ours.

If you are not aware that the way you carry yourself influences your horse, you will miss out on a big part of the ability to solve the problems you may encounter. And you will definitely miss out on some of the refinement in the work. Two bodies moving together can look as harmonious from the ground as in the riding. The ability to make groundwork light, elegant and playful like in a dance lies in the ability of the leading partner to communicate very subtly through the body

and energy with her partner and the partner being soft and focused, completely in tune with the leader.

With your horse, you can do groundwork from various positions. You can be in the basic position; walking backward in front of your horse. Or maybe you prefer to walk on the inside of your horse beside his shoulder. Or maybe you prefer more distance and do lunging or long-reining. Anywhere around your horse your body, the direction of your energy, the rhythm of your walk will influence your horse. Horses are fantastic in following examples. If you walk gently and in balance, so will your horse. If you walk unevenly, so will they. You have comparable parts: put your body in the shape, rhythm and direction of movement you would like from your horse. Do what you would like your horse to do. Be aware that you are not unconsciously doing things that you don't want your horse to do, like dropping your back, pushing stiff legs backward or bracing your neck or jaw.

Here are some ideas to help you to become aware of your habits and help set good examples for your horse.

First, consider your posture: are all your body parts 'stacked up' on top of each other? Imagine how you would like your horse to walk: we want him searching forward-down, over the back, with the maximum length from tail to ears. For our body; we have to make the translation from horizontal (the horse's spine) to vertical (our spine). So, to show the horse what we want, we have to lengthen our spine in the vertical direction; our head up, our tail bone pointing down. When all our body parts are correctly aligned, we need very limited muscle tone to keep balance. We can use our muscles to move freely. When body parts are not aligned, we need additional muscle tension to keep our body together. This limits the freedom of movement and makes us stiff and, in the worst case, it makes us sore. Classic examples are hollow backs and heads that are carried in front of the neck instead of on top of our cervical spine. The same goes for our horses; when their spines are not aligned and lengthened, their hind legs cannot swing through to lift their chests.

Another important part to consider is how you use your eyes. Quite often when we do groundwork and walk backward in front of our horse, we are so focused on getting the bending right, the inside hind leg step under, the outside shoulder in, preventing the inside shoulder from falling in, and so on, that we end up walking around with eyes fixed on a certain part of the horse. Often the inside hind leg. If you were the horse, would you come to a predator that is staring at you? Can a prey animal relax in these circumstances? Would you follow a leader that is holding the breath and has high muscle tone? Or would you prefer to walk toward a two-legged creature that is soft, breathing and sees the whole world?

The way you use your eyes can have a great effect on your breathing. As our muscles can only fully relax when we exhale, it is important to breathe deeply, to use the full volume of our lungs and have long exhalations. The same applies to our horses! Muscle tension can prevent deep breathing. And deep breathing can release muscle tension. It is important to keep breathing deeply so our horses can breathe deeply too. See if you can breathe together. You will improve your flow together.

The clearest way to ask your horse for anything is to know what you want and put it into your own body first. When it comes to groundwork, we see many people finding it hard to walk backward in a circle. They lose their sense of direction and the circle loses shape. Of course, then they also lose the shoulders of their horse. Then, they get so distracted, trying to correct the shoulders with the whip as both an inside and outside rein aid that they lose their direction completely. How is your horse supposed to walk a balanced circle if you can't do the same? It helps to imagine that you are walking backward on railroad tracks. Your horse's front legs and hind legs should be walking on the same tracks. The clearer you can show your horse by your walk where the tracks are, and in what direction they are going, the easier it is for your horse to follow you. When it is really hard, imagine you have a piece of string or elastic band tied to the back of your waistline. And this string is pulling you backward, by the waist, over the railroad tracks. This helps you keep a clear sense of direction. When walking beside your horse, imagine your railroad tracks are running parallel to your horse's

tracks. At the same distance from each other, but all the time running parallel, in the same direction of movement. The moment your railroad tracks run in a different direction as your horse's, you will disrupt his movement and either push him over the outside shoulder, or let him fall in.

Consider that when you do groundwork with a Shetland pony, the horse will mainly see your knees and feet, whereas when you work with a big warmblood, the horse is more likely to look at your shoulders. Therefore, it makes sense to be consistent in the direction of movement in all your body parts and to consider the size of the horse you work with to decide which body part you may eventually want to emphasize this in.

Another important factor in using yourself correctly while doing groundwork with your horse is the concept of being grounded. Being grounded is sometimes hard to describe but it is very easy to feel. When you stand grounded, you are balanced and stable. You radiate self-confidence and are less likely to be pushed over. When walking with a horse, we should maintain this feeling at all times. So this is a good place to write about HOW you should walk. If you have ever practiced tai-chi, then you are familiar with the tai-chi walk or rice-paper walk. This is essentially the most balanced and stable way you can walk. The idea is to always have your full weight on a foot on the ground. Most of us rush too much in walking and have formed the habit of pushing ourselves forward when we move. Just like our horses with too much push in their hind legs, we allow our weight to fall forward and catch it with the next step. This always creates a moment of instability, stiffness and tension. A balanced walk is a collected walk. Just like we want our horses to place more weight on their hind legs, bend their joints and move their legs forward before placing weight on them, we should first move one foot forward, then transfer our weight to that foot and only then move the other foot forward. We can do the same when walking backward in front of our horses.

When we put all these elements together, we are balanced in our bodies, soft in our vision and breathing, and grounded. We have a clear picture

of what we want and where we want to go. We can feel that our true strength and movement lies in our **center.** By positioning ourselves in the correct way with our tailbone down and balanced on our feet, we are stable yet flexible, ready to move in all directions at all time like a dancer or a martial artist. It is from our center that we invite our horse to join us in groundwork. Now, when we walk backward in front of a horse, we sometimes encounter pushy horses or horses that are hesitant in coming to us. We can solve this from our center. When our basics are OK, we can decide in which direction our energy goes from our center. Walking backward with a pushy horse, sometimes we send energy to the horse to block him from coming forward too much. With hesitant horses, our energy should invite the horse to come to us, so we retract a bit in our center, bringing the energy back. A nice way to practice this is with a stick of about 1 meter (3-4 feet) long, because we can feel the direction of energy through it. Ultimately, a connection through a loose rein or in liberty works according to the same principle! Do this exercise with a partner: take the stick and both you and your partner place one end of the stick in the palm of an open hand. Without holding the stick by tensing your hand or fingers, you can keep the stick up together. Now, you can decide that one of you is leading and the other is following. Let all your movements originate from your center, travel through your body and into the stick. As the leader, feel how little you need when you move from your center. As the follower, feel how all you need to do is keep the connection. The more connected you are with yourself and the better your leader moves from her center, the easier it is to follow all movements without stiffness or tension. From the outside, it becomes impossible to determine who is the leader and who is the follower, as the movement flows harmoniously.

Want to feel how centered you really are? Then place the broomstick under your navel and connect directly center to center. Can you still move together, without dropping the broomstick and without tension? When you have experience this connection with a human partner, bring that feeling into the groundwork you do with your horse. Or even better, bring this feeling into every aspect of your life! Whether you connect with other humans or horses, the centered and grounded approach will cost you less energy and bring you a gentler result.

The Spiraling Spine

One of the most valuable things I can offer riders is to teach you how to spiral your spine. As horses move horizontally and we sit vertically, there is a difference in how we use our spine compared to our horses. In our hips and legs we follow the rotation of our horse's spine. This movement travels up into our spine, where it results in a spiraling movement when we ride turns or side movements. It makes our shoulders move with the shoulders of our horse. When the outside shoulder of the horse comes forward, the outside of our torso (the outside ribs, shoulder and ear) come forward. When the outside shoulder of the horse moves back, we go back to being straight. You can imagine this movement as a corkscrew, a pepper mill or a spiraling staircase.

This spiral starts in the outside hind leg of the horse. When that leg stands on the ground, it pushes the outside ribs of the horse up. We receive this push in our outside stirrup and seat bone. This is where our spiral starts. Try to turn while you walk in place. On a trampoline is even better, as the trampoline gives you an upward push. You will notice that you can turn more easily with your inside leg up and your outside leg standing on the ground. When you try to turn with your outside leg in the air, you will feel that you have less space to turn and it will twist your standing inside knee.

When we ride a turn or increase the bend in our horse, we ask the horse's shoulders to turn in. By spiraling our spine in more, we bring the outside of our rib cage more forward and in. This brings our shoulders, arms and hands in. This results in an opening inside rein and an outside rein that touches against the neck of the horse. The spiraling in our spine and the resulting action of the rein makes the horse turn or increase the bend by bringing his shoulders in. Whether the horse turns or bends toward a shoulder-in depends on the action of our hips and leg.

The best exercise to practice spiraling your spine is to ride a circle. It is a continuous turn. On each step, the horse's outside shoulder must turn in a bit. On each step we have the same spiral, back-to-neutral spiral again action in our spine. Like the turning of a pepper mill. Then, make

the circle smaller by spiraling a bit more in each step. This makes the horse turn his shoulders more in, decreasing the size of the circle. When you make the circle bigger, do not spiral out. We want the horse to go in the same bend, whether you make the circle bigger or smaller. We do not want to counter-bend the horse in this circle. So to make the circle bigger, continue to spiral in, but use the inside leg in rhythm with the horse's inside hind leg in a downward motion to send the inside hind leg of your horse forward and in and under his point of weight to make the circle bigger.

(For the correct movement of the inside leg, see 'The Swipe')

When you have found your spiral and your horse responds to it, you can also ride your spiraling spine on a straight line, which results in shoulder-in. In fact, you will discover that in all side movements, the spiraling spine is the key to remain in flow with your horse.

The Pelvis and the True Core

To position your pelvis and spine in the correct position and allow your body to move with the movement of your horse, we use muscles. The final result is of course different for each rider because we are all shaped differently, but we all have the same bones and the same muscles. To help you achieve the correct posture, riding instructors often use verbal instructions and/or visualizations, such as "sit on your tail," "pull your miniskirt down," "sit on your pants pockets," and "sit deeper in the saddle."

What we as riding instructors are looking for is to find the instruction that helps you, the rider, to find the right feeling and experience. For me, I get the right result in my pelvis and spine when I think of a little weight hanging down from my tail bone. For some of my students, however, that means nothing to them. When we try to achieve the right position without having the right experience or feeling behind it (imagine your instructor positioning you in the saddle in the 'correct' position and then telling you to keep this posture), we often end up trying to hold the posture with our 'outside' muscles. The results are stiff, inflexible and it gets hard to breathe. As soon as we stop trying, our body wants to move back to its old position.

But which muscles should we use and which should we keep relaxed while we ride? And if we know which muscles we want to use, how do we get our brain to signal to these specific muscles and not to others? The task at hand for riding instructors is as difficult as it is for someone to explain to another person how to wiggle your ears.

My teacher, Tom Nagel, helped me tremendously to understand the concept of tone versus tension. In his books and clinics he describes how riders can learn to engage their psoas muscles to stabilize their seat while keeping flexibility. When we learn to engage our psoas we are stable in our seat without any tension in our abdominal muscles. This is true core stability yet allows riders to breathe deeply into their center. Tense your stomach muscles while you read this sentence and at the same time try to breathe deeply into your belly. It doesn't work, does it?

Experienced riders use their psoas to stabilize and move on their horses, often without knowing what they are doing. Using instructions such as "sit deep into the saddle", "center yourself" and "sit on your pants pockets" they try to describe what they experience when they engage their true core. However, if their students follow these instructions without truly realizing what they are after, some may use their outside muscles to create the same picture: tensing their abdominals to put their pelvis in the right position. It may look the same but it does not feel the same and does not give you the same stable flexibility and space to breathe.

Therefore, I agree with Tom Nagel that understanding and being aware of the psoas is the missing link for many riders. I am happy to see that the knowledge about the psoas is spreading among the horse-riding community these days. In Tom's book 'Zen and Horseback Riding' you can find some interesting exercises to become more aware of your psoas, your 'true core'.

Seat Bones for Him and Her

The pelvis of men and women are shaped differently. In women, the entire pelvis is wider and the seat bones are further apart. Also, the angle at which the pubic bones join in the front of the pelvis is different in women. It causes women to have a pubic arch that is U-shaped, while in men this is V-shaped. The reason why the shape of the female pelvis is different than the male pelvis is to allow for child birth. The pelvis of a man is narrower and the iliac crest is higher. This allows for better bipedal movement. The interesting thing is that there is a dilemma here in the development of the male and female pelvis. If a female pelvis became any wider, making child birth easier, she would no longer be able to walk. But the optimal pelvis for walking, like the male pelvis, is too narrow for child birth. The pelvis of a woman is therefore something like a compromise between correct movement and allowing babies to be born without too many complications.

This difference between the male and female pelvis also affects the positioning of the pelvis in the saddle. As the seat bones in the female pelvis are 2 to 3 centimeters further apart, this means that the seat of the saddle supporting the seat bones must be wider for women then for male seat bones. Also, the angle of the pubic bone in women means that women have more problems with a high front pommel, especially when it is combined with a narrow deep seat. But, as most saddles are made by men, there are a lot of saddles 'out there' that are not compatible with a female pelvis. When the seat of the saddle is too narrow, it makes the seat bones drop on the sides of the seat. This causes the pelvis to balance not on the seat bones, but on the pubic bone instead. The female rider will end up sitting on her crotch instead of on her seat bones and may experience pain and even chafing.

The correct way to sit in a saddle is balanced on the seat bones. Then, a rider can decide to come forward over the seat bones toward a light seat or to roll further back on the seat bones for a collected seat. If a rider is not balanced over her seat bones, but sits in a saddle where the seat bones drop to the side, the possibility of rolling over the seat bones is

gone and extreme pressure gets put on the pubic bone. No one can feel comfortable or remain flexible in such a situation.

Nowadays, there are special saddles that are designed to fit the female pelvis. My recommendation is to always go for a saddle with a flat seat that allows you to balance on your seat bones. Find a saddle that has enough space between the front and back pommel so you can position your pelvis in the middle. But most important is to feel comfortable. Take some expert eyes along to help you find a saddle that fits both your horse and your own body!

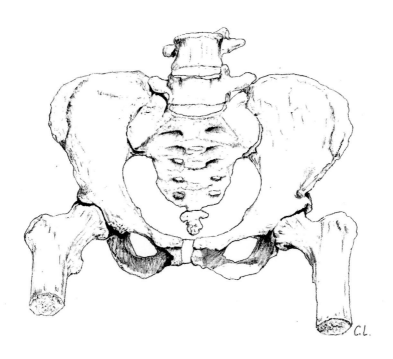

Move to Sit Still!

Ever had a riding instructor tell you to keep your hands or legs or head or any other body part still while riding? Did it work for you? In my experience, when you try to keep something still, you brace yourself against the movement of your horse. It is impossible to sit still on a moving horse as with each stride of his hind legs he will swing his back. This movement needs to pass through your body and move out through your head, arms and legs. Any joint you try to keep still will block this movement and create friction in your body. That is uncomfortable for you and your horse.

Now of course the other extreme is when a rider is too loose and all their body parts shake in all directions. This is not stable and not pleasant for horse and rider either. The ideal is to have all joints moving in a toned way, channeling the energy in the right directions together with the movement of the horse. When you move with the horse, it will feel stable and flexible and it will look as if you are sitting still. On a horse with big movements, that means your movements will be big. And to move that much, to release your body so much as to follow these movements, that may feel scary to some people in the beginning. That is why many people may try to hold their horses back, asking them for smaller movements and consciously or unconsciously making their horse's back stiff so that they don't have to move so much in their seat. There is even a trend now for breeding horses that are leg movers (horses that do not move their back in relation to their legs) as these quiet backs are 'easier to sit on'. Instead of creating horses with stiff backs though, I plead for training riders with flexible hip joints. It is healthier for the horses and also for us!

As children, we are all more flexible. We loose flexibility when we get older because of our life styles, our formed habits and the physical changes we go through as we mature. Growing older with bad habits creates back problems, migraines and all other sorts of pain and discomfort. Do we really want to adjust the world around us to fit our sore stiff bodies to the point where even our horses have to adapt to our disabilities, rather than working on our bodies and increasing our

abilities? In my experience with working peoples' bodies, we can still reverse a lot of the 'acquired' junk in our bodies. In my travels I have met students who are the living examples that yes, you can change. Once I met a 79-year-old rider who had the kind of moving hips I hardly see even in 25 year olds. When I asked her how she got to be so supple at her age she answered, "I started doing yoga when I was 69 years old." I would not have put her anything above 58 from how she looked and in her riding movements she surpassed all the young people in that clinic by far.

So, yes, we can all become more flexible. No need for excuses like "this is just the way I am." All soft tissue is changeable up to the day we die. It is just a matter of will, training and bodywork.

Now, back to riding. The moment we block a joint somewhere our entire body will stiffen and we will block the movement of the horse. So in the beginning: exaggerate. Do more. Then, once the movement has become a pattern in your brain, do less, give it direction, think it and allow it. But never stop it!

Breathing in All Directions

When we learn to ride and start practicing other awareness methods such as yoga or tai chi, sooner or later we get confronted with our breathing. As children, we have a natural vertical alignment in our posture. How else could we learn to get up and walk, if not for being able to balance our disproportionately large-sized skull on top of our little bodies? With this correct posture comes correct breathing. Most young children have beautifully balanced breathing that includes both the chest and the abdominal area.

Over time, as we grow up, our furniture, sitting in school, cell phones and slouching on the couch ruins our natural vertical alignment. This, combined with our 'monkey-brains' that are thinking and stressing all the time, affects our breathing. Apparently, one quarter of the western population suffers from mild to severe hyperventilation, a medical breathing specialist once told me in hospital (after I'd been diagnosed with mild hyperventilation). Most of us have ruined our posture, making it impossible for our lungs to function properly. After I began working on my posture and breathing, my breathing slowed down and I started to get more air per inhale. The best measurable effect of this training I see in my scuba diving: I can go far longer on a tank of air than I used to and nowadays I often come up with more bars left on my air gauge than my diving buddies. In the old days, I used to be the first to surface because I'd run out of air.

It makes sense that our posture affects our breathing, as our body is the vessel in which our lungs expand and contract. When our bodies are slouched, crooked or otherwise restricted, it reduces the ability of our lungs to expand to their maximum.

Our lungs are like two giant balloons. When they fill with air they should expand in all directions. When they fill up they expand downward with the help of our diaphragm. The diaphragm pushes our organs in our abdominal cavity forward. This creates a lower belly that moves forward on the inhale. Our gut makes room for our lungs to expand down. This is what we call 'abdominal breathing'. When our abdominal muscles are heavily trained they become shorter and stiffer. Then our abdominal muscles have a hard time letting our belly move forward. In

other words: a six-pack reduces your capacity for abdominal breathing. In my clinics I always joke that "in riding, a Buddha belly is preferred over a six-pack." Many female riders have sighed from relief over those words. But it is no joke. We affect our breathing tremendously with our crazy notion of tight stomachs, six-packs and bodies 'hard as rock'. The abdominal muscles are not designed to be tight. They are designed to keep our intestines in and allow for movement.

Our lungs expand not only downward when they fill with air, they also expand on both sides and upward. As our lungs are encased by our ribcage, which protects them from injury, our ribcage has to expand on each inhale. This is possible thanks to the cartilage connections between our ribs and our sternum and because of the joints that connect our ribs to our spine. We have various different muscles attached to our ribs. All these muscles need to contract and expand when we breathe. Often I encounter people with so much tension in these muscles that their rib cage is stuck. The less your rib cage can expand, the less room your lungs have to expand. This compression of the lungs leads to many lung- and breathing problems. The expansion in the ribcage, especially up into your chest, is often referred to as 'chest breathing'. This is often considered a bad thing. But only if you breathe shallow without combining your chest breathing with your belly breathing!

We need to allow our lungs to expand in all directions: down, to the side and up. This means our muscles need to allow this movement. When they are stuck, movement and therefore breathing is reduced. The more the expansion is reduced, the more breaths per minute you need to obtain sufficient oxygen in your blood and to excrete the CO_2 your body produces. If you can use your lungs to the fullest, you can do with fewer breaths.

We need both abdominal and chest breathing for full use of our lungs. The one is not better than the other. If you have good breathing, you will breathe down and then expand your lungs to the sides and up. My teacher, Tom Nagel, calls this 'vertical breathing'. With correct up-and-down breathing like this, you can maintain your correct posture without effort. And at the same time, your ribs expand to the back, to the sides and to the front. You become wider, longer and more stable at the same time!

Breathe into Your Half Halt

The half halt is probably one of the most mysterious things in riding. There are so many explanations, so many ideas, and so many applications. Let's try to simplify it as much as possible, because seen from my perspective, it's really not necessary to have so much confusion about it.

A half halt is a 'get ready' signal to the horse. It is used to rebalance the horse (bring the weight more to his hind quarter and bend his haunches). Doing this makes the horse is freer in the shoulders and better able to do upward and downward transitions, turns, side movements and so on. Basically, we rebalance the horse every time we want to start something new. But also while continuing the same exercise we use the half halt to rebalance the horse each time it starts to tip its weight toward the shoulders. A series of half halts brings the horse into a collected state.

The half halt is traditionally described as a nearly imperceptible aid from the rider, involving the seat, hand and leg. Hand and leg are engaged automatically, when the rider uses his seat correctly. Different ways to describe the use of the seat in a half halt include 'collect yourself', 'drop your tail', 'pull up your pants zipper', 'bring your pubic bone up', 'Das kreuz anziehen (German)' or 'brace your back'. But as with all words, there are different interpretations to these instructions. And here I go, using even more words, to try to describe what they all really mean. When you imagine the 'shape' of the pelvis you want to achieve in the half halt, it would be to bring the front of the pelvis slightly up and the back-end slightly down. It straightens the lower back out of its natural curve, feeling like a very slight rounding of the back. If you try to do this with your outside muscles, however, you could tense your stomach and/or your butt, or you could collapse in your spine and round yourself too much, ending up in a slumped position.

The correct way to execute this movement is by engaging the psoas muscles in the pelvis while maintaining your vertical alignment. But if you are not sure how to find your psoas, the easiest way to give half-halts is through breathing. In an earlier article I referred to Tom Nagel's

term 'vertical breathing'. He also writes that every inhalation is, in fact, a half halt. Each time you inhale in, you allow your diaphragm to drop, and your tail drops slightly at the same time. Then, when your lungs fill with air, you create lift in your spine and your ribcage expands all around. This rebalances you and lengthens your spine. While inhaling, if your upper arms hang down relaxed and your hands float gently up from bent elbows, dropping your tail creates a slight pushing sensation through the arms (also see 'Pushing hands'). This is the 'hand' aid we need in the half halt that pushes the horse's ears away from us and encourages the horse to search for the riders hands by stretching the upper line.

Also, the same inhalation tones the iliopsoas attachment on the inside of our upper legs and tones the other adductors in that area. The result will feel as if the flesh on the inside of the upper leg gets 'sucked up' a little bit, inviting the horse to lift its back.

So, then, if every inhalation is in fact a half halt; what to do with the exhalation? Simple: on each one you can do an 'action', either a transition upward or downward, a turn or the start of a side movement. Or simply tell your horse, "Keep doing what you are doing."

How do you ride up or downward transitions with these kind of half halts? Inhale and rebalance yourself (and through that, your horse). Then, for the transition up: change the rhythm of your seat to the new gait you desire, and apply lower leg if necessary. Never start to push or tense in your seat or leg, as it inhibits your breathing and the horse's movement. If the horse does not follow your change of rhythm, gently encourage him with your whip behind your leg and reward when you get the desired response.

For the downward transition: inhale and rebalance, exhale and slow your rhythm down into the desired rhythm. If the horse does not follow your downward transition, give gentle squeezes on both reins (opening and closing your fingers like squeezing water out of a sponge), but continue a forward push through the arms. If you pull on the reins, the backward movement will block the forward step of the hind legs, raise the horse's

head and drop his back. Some horses will refuse to stop in this position, so encourage the forward movement of the hind legs and the rounding of his back. Repeat this inhale-exhale-squeeze as often as necessary, but with clear intent on the squeeze if the horse walks through the aids. Take your time to explain the meaning. Do not block your hips while applying more rein. Keep the hips moving in the desired rhythm, thus giving a clear rhythm for the horse to follow.

How do you collect a horse using half halts? If the horse is relaxed with forward-stepping hind legs and a nice energy and round upper line, the collection (bringing more weight to the hind quarter and bending his haunches) is nothing more than a sequence of half halts, moving more and more weight back. Never ask for more than the horse can follow, never do it longer than the horse can keep at it. Go back to forward-down as soon as you feel any stiffness or tension in your horse.

Pushing Hands

Pushing hands is a training routine in the Chinese martial arts that teaches students the concepts of sensitivity, timing, coordination and energy, among other things. Pushing hands teaches a student to allow the body to yield to force, redirecting it rather than resisting it with strength. Our natural instinct is to resist force with force. When somebody pushes against us, we often stiffen to resist the pressure. When we stiffen, we lose our balance. When we are centered and relaxed, we can yield while remaining stable and grounded. The metaphor of bamboo in the wind is often used to describe this concept. The bamboo is strong yet flexible. It moves with the wind instead of resisting it, and because of that quality, it doesn't break and always bounces back upright after being bent.

The pushing hands exercise from tai chi can teach us valuable lessons that we can apply to riding.

We all know horses that fall on the shoulders, 'grab the bit', and put weight on the reins. It feels like the horse is pulling on the rider's hands. The rider's reflex can be to hold or even pull back. This tenses up the rider and requires a lot of strength in the arms. There are even some 'rider fitness' training programs that advise riders to work out their arms just to be able to 'hold' this pull on the reins. With a rider pulling on the reins in a response to an out-of-balance horse, the horse stiffens too, and puts even more weight on the bit. This results in a horse that is even more out of balance, which requires even more strength in the rider's arms, and so on.

When a rider simply lets the reins slide through the hands when the horse pulls on the bit, making no contact, the end result could be that the horse gets more and more out of balance. I have seen horses that are so unbalanced that they just keep on going faster and faster. Like an object rolling down a flight of stairs, once it starts to fall, it will continue to do so and accelerate on the way down.

From a biomechanical point of view, we can very simply explain the tendency of some horses to put weight on the bit. It starts with a

backward push in the hind legs, which unbalances the horse and pushes the horse's weight forward. Before a horse puts weight in the rider's hands, he has already put his weight on his shoulders. And it is here that the horizontal balance of the horse is lost. The solution is not to hold against the pressure with the reins, or to make no contact at all. The solution is to rebalance the horse and rider together. Engage the horse's hind legs to step forward and take the weight so he can lift and free his shoulders.

Rather than having a horse and rider pull against each other on both ends of a rein, or a rider dropping the rein and losing all contact, we can use the basics of pushing hands to increase both the horse's and rider's sensitivity and improve the rider's timing and coordination in giving half halts through the reins to rebalance the horse and move his weight from the shoulders to the hind quarter. This brings the horse back into horizontal balance. And a horizontally balanced horse is light in contact on the rein.

The basic idea is simple: just like in the tai chi version of pushing hands, it is all about the connection of your arms and hands to your center. The energy from your center flows through your arms, out of your hands and through the reins to your horse's head. This constant flow of energy is what lengthens his neck and helps him come over his back. The principle only works when your seat is correct: when your pelvis is vertical, your psoas muscles are engaged and your spine is aligned properly. In other words, without a balanced center, there is no energetic push in the arms.

When the horse tends to 'dive down' and put weight in the hands of the rider, the rider should think of bringing her pubic bone slightly up toward her nose and at the same time send her energetic push of her arms forward and up toward her horse's ears. This is a subtle thing, the elbows do not come away from the body; it is just a slight bend in the elbows coming from the center. So instead of resisting the pull of the horse by pulling back, the rider changes the direction of energy and uses the unbalance of the horse as an opportunity to rebalance the both of them. It is a short, quick movement, and when done in exact timing,

this is the half halt that will rebalance the horse. When the breath is used correctly, this works even better (see: Breathe into Your Half Halt).

The pushing hands exercise in the martial arts is all about learning to find your opponent's opening. That short moment where your training partner is out of balance. In that moment, you can strike and with a push or a quick pull, you can make the other lose his footing. Horses know how to play this game too. In a moment when you are somewhere else in your mind, where you stiffen up or have no connection though the reins, they have the opening to do something unexpected. The most classic example is the horse diving down to eat a quick bite of grass, pulling the rider out of the seat. The connection from your center through your arms and through the reins to the horse's head is the best way for the horse to feel if you are 'there' or not. By pushing energy from your center to his head, you leave him no openings he can take advantage of. By pulling, because it unbalances and tenses you, you basically give him an opening all the time, and instead of a game of sensitivity, it becomes a war in which force is met with force. And what is achieved by force will always be less elegant, less pleasant and less harmonious for both.

By pushing, you maintain an energetic connection. You feel the other and the other feels you. You can extend the horse's upper line, allowing the hind legs to come forward. Just imagine lengthening your own 'upper line', which is your spine. With your tail dropping down and your head flowing forward and up, your pushing hands energy will be easy to find.

Want to practice it by yourself? Use a wall or a partner. Place your feet apart at hip width, with one foot in front of the other. Bend your knees slightly, relax your upper body. Center and ground yourself. Make loose fists as if you are holding the reins and place them against the wall or against your partner's palms. Let the energy from your center come through your arms and out of your fists. Can you push into the wall or partner from your center? When you increase the energy flow, can you feel how this grounds and centers you even more? Can you maintain breathing and relaxation? Then you have found your pushing hands!

'The Swipe'

In most riders, one of the most common dysfunctional habits is kicking the legs backward. It comes from having learned that the 'forward driving' aid means kicking the lower leg into the horse's stomach. This movement shortens the entire leg of the rider. The muscles in the back of the calf and the hamstrings shorten and stiffen. It usually also tilts a rider forward in the pelvis, arching the back.

Some riders have learned to do this with two legs at the same time, to make the horse go forward. In response, however, I usually see horses go even slower, as they brace themselves against the rider's heels and legs. When using both legs at once, the rider loses the bilateral movement in her hips. As the movement of the horse's hind legs and back is bilateral, using both legs at the same time makes no sense. A horse is not a kangaroo! We send one hind leg forward, then the other. This keeps the horse's spine swinging and the rider's body intact, giving the horse a chance to increase rhythm and energy.

In a turn, circle or side movement, I use the inside leg aid to make the horse hollow around my inside seat and leg and to bring his inside hip forward so his inside hind leg can swing forward under the point of weight. When I want the inside hind leg of my horse to go forward and further in under his point of weight, I give the horse my inside leg aid the moment the inside hind leg is in the air. This is the moment when the horse's back swings down on the inside. It is the moment I feel my inside upper leg drop. Dropping my inside leg is natural and causes my inside lower leg to lengthen. It 'sweeps' my lower leg forward at the same time.

The idea behind the inside leg aid to bend a horse is to enhance the horse's natural movement. In the moment when the inside hind leg is stepping forward and in, ask the horse to do just a little bit more. Thus, the only thing you need to do with your leg is just a little bit more of what you are already doing! The entire leg lengthens and the lower leg brushes against the horse's coat, from back to front along the stomach. I call this movement 'the swipe'.

When a rider uses the traditional aid of kicking back with the lower leg, the inside hip comes up instead of down. The rider's movement blocks and works against the natural swing of the horse's back. It then blocks the forward-and-in movement of the inside hind leg. Then, because the horse stiffens and shortens, the rider tends to apply more leg, resulting only in a stiffer horse. To prevent the horse from bracing and allow the natural movement of the horse to improve, the rider should maintain her natural movement and stay in rhythm with her horse. Mastering the swipe will give you the tool to do so.

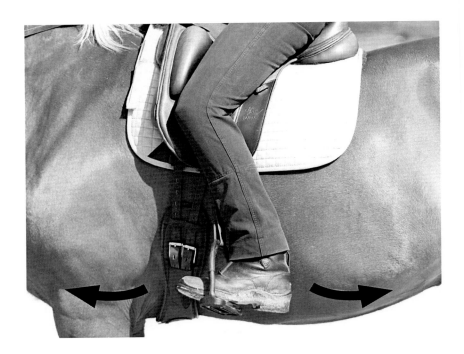

Wag Your Tail!

The light seat is a way of sitting 'above' the horse which I use for young horses and horses with weak backs. When a rider sits heavily into the back of a horse, that makes him drop his back easily. The weight of the seat bones pressing down into the back muscles or the weight of the pillows of the saddle pressing down can be enough for a horse to drop the back. Using the light seat, we can take our seat bones out off of the horse's back and remove this pressure off of the horse's back muscles. Of course, we are not actually getting any lighter from sitting in a light seat. It is all about placing the weight elsewhere. In the light seat we can displace our weight through our upper legs and knees onto the rib cage of the horse. The ribs cover a huge surface and can carry us without making the horse drop its back. In the light seat with a saddle, it is important not to put the weight on the stirrups, because that will press the saddle down into the back muscles. The light seat is also a great way to teach a rider to separate the movement of the left and right hip and upper leg. It is therefore the perfect way to teach 'bouncing' riders how to sit through the trot.

The light seat is used while riding the horse forward and down. It encourages the horse to relax his upper line and that allows the *schwung* to come from the hindquarters into the spine of the horse. The hind legs will be able to swing further through under the horse, resulting in longer, more carrying strides and more shoulder freedom. Using the light seat the rider should be aware of not pressing the shoulders of the horse too much down. This happens when the rider takes his weight forward too much. In the beginning, just on introducing this exercise to horses that have strong front legs, it is not such a big problem because the first goal is to get the upper line stretched, but later on we want the shoulder to become lighter and the rider should focus more on stretching the neck forward rather than the downward direction of the head.

When rising out of the saddle and up on the upper legs, the rider should still be able to follow the three-dimensional swing of the horse's ribcage. This means that just like in a normal vertically aligned seat, the hips and upper legs must be free and moveable. This is possible when the rider

folds in the hip joint and uses their hip, knee and ankle joints to follow the movement of the horse. When the rider takes a light seat with an arched back or while pressing the heels down, the quality of movement in hip, knee and ankles joints decreases. Therefore, in the light seat the rider should still aim at lengthening and rounding her own upper line, filling out the lower back, and keeping all joints free and moveable.

The exercise I have many riders do is to feel the movement of the horse's back in this light seat in walk and trot. It helps tremendously in developing a good sitting trot to first learn to separate both legs while having the seat bones out of the saddle in light seat. Most people start to post when they get uncomfortable in the sitting trot, but posting makes you move both of your hips forward at the same time and does not help you to find your left-right separation. The light seat is the key 'in between' exercise to improve sitting the trot. Of course, you must first find the correct alignment in your seat, before you can move. With your upper body folding forward and up from the hip joints, your knees hinge and your feet and lower legs should be slightly back to find the proper balance. Remember that when you are not in balance, you may fall back into the saddle, which is not comfortable for your horse. So, in the beginning, hold onto your horse's mane or the front of your saddle until you are sure you have found your balance. When you can stay up comfortably, start off in the walk and find the left-right movement of your horse's back in your upper legs. When you are comfortable, move on to the trot. Notice that the left-right movement makes you bend one leg at the time. This movement makes your imaginary tail wag a little to the left and to the right. Be careful not to lift your tail up, but keep your tail bone pointing into the seat of your saddle, about 2cm (1 inch) out of the saddle. When the tail bone points down, your pelvis is still engaged and your lower back is filled out. With your tail bone pointing more up, we get a so-called 'duck seat' with a hollow back and the seat bones sticking backwards out too much. In the latter seat, the movement of hips, knees and ankles is restricted and it is harder to find the left-right separation.

In the correct light seat, the left-right swing that you have in your legs and hips makes the muscles of your lower back more supple, so that the

swing can travel all the way through your spine just like in a normal vertical alignment. Also in this seat, the movement comes out the top of your skull and makes your nose 'wag' just like your tail bone. A correct light seat not only makes it easier for the horse to move and stretch his back muscles underneath you, it also gives you a free massage of your back muscles and should help release tension in your own spine.

On longer rides, especially out in the forest when doing longer stretches of trot, I recommend the light seat as the easiest way to move with your horse. You may feel funny 'wagging your tail', but it has a beneficial effect on both you and your horse!

The Making of a Good Rider

It is much nicer and easier to sit on a well-developed horse than on a crooked, stiff horse. This is why we should not develop only the rider and train only the seat. When a rider takes lessons with their own horse we should also work on developing the horse. The two should go hand in hand. As the horse gradually improves and becomes stronger, the rider can sit more nicely and move more gently. And the more softly the rider sits, the more finesse the rider can put into the aids and make the communication with the horse more and more subtle, improving the horse's shape and balance.

As an instructor or trainer, it is important to define what our goals are for our horses, our pupils and their horses. We should first clarify the difference in teaching beginning and more experienced riders. When we teach a beginning rider, then we strive to teach them a balanced, independent seat and proper feeling into the horse. It is best done using a well-balanced school horse on the lunge. We do not focus on teaching the rider to influence the horse. We teach the rider to have a soft, independent seat and feel movements of the horse in all the different gaits.

When we teach a higher level rider we focus more on the use of different aids in order to develop the horse. It is not so much training a rider but training a trainer. Using exercises to strengthen the horse and develop it symmetrically, we can use body awareness techniques to keep the rider connected to their body and prevent them from losing feeling in using the aids. If an experienced rider has not had proper body awareness education when they learned to ride, somewhere during the further training they will reach a point where they need more body awareness to change something in themselves in order to improve the horse. Then the rider needs to come back to basic seat training to change habits and movement patterns. This is one of the reasons why professional classical riders still spend time on the lunge every week, training their seat.

The beginning rider

Ideally, with a novice rider, we should work on the basics, teaching the rider to have a nice, balanced seat, and not hinder the horse. To get out of the horse's way so that it can move freely. The rider should be guided in developing the feeling into the horse at all times in all gaits and be relaxed in the seat. When the novice has learned to be in balance, only then can we start to teach basic aids for transitions and changes in direction without the rider disturbing the horse's movement.

The problem I face is that novice riders who have not yet developed the right feel and proper balance are often riding inexperienced, poorly trained or unbalanced horses. It is almost impossible to teach a rider to simply sit, feel and relax on a horse that cannot go forward in a balanced, relaxed manner. These horses need a rider who can support the horse through their seat and make it carry the rider in a healthy way. Since all horses are born with some asymmetry in their bodies, carrying the weight of the rider can make them stiff and cause them injuries. Therefore, an inexperienced rider should always be taught how to ride on an educated, supple, well-carrying horse. Inexperienced horses should be trained by well-balanced riders.

In the Renaissance, when riding was only for well-fortuned noble men, this was exactly the case: riding was taught using 'professors': highly schooled horses of age 16 and up that taught the rider the perfect feeling and seat. These horses were usually first moved in place and later on the lunge and riders learned to sit in perfect balance. After this seat training (that could take up to 2 years and is still done (in some extent) in the traditional schools in Europe), riders began learning the aids. Finally, when the feeling and balance of the rider had developed enough, they would move on to training younger, less-experienced horses. Because the riders had already experienced the end product; the perfect feeling of a well-moving horse, they could slowly train the young horses with their seat and aids to gain horizontal balance and collection. Their school master had given them a blueprint for balance, suppleness and collection, which they could then pass on to their young horses. Unfortunately we usually do not have the luxury to be seat-trained first on a professor horse anymore. With most combinations we immediately

have to teach the rider how to ride the horse properly so that the horse has fewer problems in carrying the rider. This means we skip parts of the important basics.

As an instructor I find it very important to select experienced riding horses for beginning riders. Horses that have the strong hindquarter and back that can support unbalanced riders without causing too much damage to themselves. These horses also need to be exercised by experienced riders to maintain their strong backs and hindquarters and prevent deterioration.

If such horses are not available, for example if a student has only one horse and does not have the opportunity to ride another, the instructor will have to teach this unexperienced rider some basic training techniques that will prevent the horse from being harmed too much. I take these riders off their horses and make them start with academic training from the ground. The novice riders will get a better idea of how the horse should move, and begins to develop some feeling through the reins or lunge. The novice learns how to use the body in guiding the horse and does not disturb the balance of the horse or ruin the back of the horse with their weight. The horse develops his body and will be able to carry the rider better later on.

The more advanced rider

Once the rider has developed a basic seat and balance, most riders have higher ambitions than just sitting comfortably and being transported. These riders want to train their horse toward higher goals, which can be found in various disciplines. However, I focus mainly on a basic education for a horse. I want my students to train their horses by teaching them how to carry a rider properly and then specialize in academic dressage. In the case of an advanced rider, the rider should be taught how to be the horse's educator. The rider needs to learn to be effective, have good timing, how to use the aids and make them more refined while teaching the horse more difficult exercises and work toward collection. If instructors have pupils like this, we need to understand in more detail how the seat can work as the rider's instrument in educating the horse toward the chosen goal. In this case there has to be a clear distinction between the disciplines since horses are taught different aids and riders have different goals in the various disciplines. However, the same basic biomechanics continues to apply to all horses and riders in all disciplines and on all levels. So even for advanced riders, basic body awareness and seat training helps teach them how to do new exercises and gives them a strong foundation on which to build the higher exercises.

A rider with a perfect seat on a badly moving horse is not a rider (read: trainer) at all, but merely being transported; a passenger looking pretty but not having much influence on the horse. To feel through the seat into the horse and then use the proper aids in seat, legs, voice and reins to improve the horse's movement and make it better, that is the challenge for all riders who want to be trainers.

The Inside Hand and Rein

The inside rein – controlled by the rider's inside hand – can have two functions. The first is that it can have a direct impact on the head of the horse. This we call the 'direct rein'. The second function is that by moving the rein sideways, touching the horse on the neck, we move the horse's shoulders out. This we call the 'indirect rein'. It is the same as in the concept of neck reining in western riding.

Of course, the outside rein can also be an indirect rein, by moving the shoulders of the horse in. We use it in turns and lateral work, such as the shoulder-in. In the chapter 'What to do with the outside rein', I describe the concept of the indirect outside rein in greater detail. In addition, the outside rein can also be a direct rein. It has the effect of reducing the bend of the neck when the horse brings its head and neck in too much.

In this chapter, I focus on the inside hand of the rider, and the distinction between the direct inside rein and the indirect inside rein.

Of course, a rider's hand never functions by itself. Or better said, it CAN function by itself (and often it does lead a life of its own), but it SHOULD never function by itself. A hand, a rein, is the extension from the rider's core. Each rein aid given should come from the rider's body and travel through the rein to influence the horse. A hand used without seat comes in without notice. It is too sudden, too abrupt, and disrupts the flow of energy through the horse. As an extension from the rider's body, the hand allows energy to flow forward, through the rein to the horse's head. This encourages the horse to seek the hand, bringing its head forward and down, and rounding its back. This allows the hind legs to come forward in under his point of weight and actively carry the rider.

Often, when I ask people to use the direct inside rein to ask for *stelling* in the horse (turning the head from the poll so that horse turns his head inward a little), I see riders bringing their inside hand closer to their belly button. They bring the inside rein closer to the horse's neck or even touch the horse's neck with it. The effect on the rider is that their

spine can no longer spiral in but rather spirals out. Their inside hand no longer flows energy forward to the head of the horse, but rather becomes a pulling hand, blocking energy and blocking the horse's inside hind leg from stepping forward under his point of weight. The effect on the horse is that they take the rein as an indirect rein rather than a direct rein. The horse then bends from where the rein touches the neck. This leads the horse to fall over the outside shoulder and pushes his inside hind leg out and back instead of swinging it forward and under. He bends his neck but his body does not join in and his back does not come up. The rein has lost its function of a direct rein asking for *stelling* and has become an indirect rein that makes the horse collapse in his neck and fall over the shoulder.

The correct way to use the direct inside rein to ask for *stelling* is to have your inside arm and hand follow the spiral of your spine. Your spine spirals in, your arms follow, your inside hand comes away from the neck. My Centered Riding® teacher Karen Irland describes it as like holding a tea pot in the inside hand, actively pouring a cup of tea toward the inside your horse's head. I like to describe it as holding a watering can, pouring water on some nice flowers that grow in front of your horse's inside shoulder. You can also think of it as simply allowing energy to flow from your pelvis, through your elbow and underarm toward the inside bit ring.

The direct inside rein should always be an OPENING rein. As if you are opening the door for your horse on the inside, allowing him to come in with his nose. If you need more from the horse, you can slightly lift the inside hand for a very short moment. You lift the hand by bending the elbow so that your inside shoulder stays down and relaxed. You lift it the spiraling in moment of your movement. This asks the horse to bring his nose in, which gives you the needed *stelling* and bending in his neck. Combined with your spiraling spine and your inside leg, this allows the entire horse to bend. It brings his inside hip and hind leg forward so your horse can engage his psoas muscles and lift his back.

It is very important to consider which aid you use with an opening rein. You can open your inside rein quite a lot, as if you are lunging yourself,

on a young horse with the rein attached to a cavesson. If you use a snaffle, you want to open only slightly to make the suggestion. Opening a lot with a snaffle can move the bit through the mouth and/or move the lower jaw of the horse to the inside, which causes a wrong rotation in the spine. Therefore, with a snaffle I prefer the tiny lift that I described above. The bit doesn't work into the lower jaw but instead gently lifts the corner of your horse's mouth.

When you use your inside hand to create an opening rein and your horse falls in, it is not the job of the inside rein to correct this. We can see this failure quite often: when the rider opens the inside rein and the horse, not used to carrying himself, falls into the opening some riders keep the inside rein close against the neck. The rein is then supposed to prevent the horse from falling in. Bringing the hand closer to the rider's belly button or the horse's withers will cause a shortening and/or over-bending of the neck. It creates a lookalike, but it ruins correct stelling and bending. It also brings the horse out of balance and shortens his stride. If the horse falls in when you open the hand and rein, it should be the inside leg that yields the horse back out and helps him find a new balance with his inside hind leg under the point of weight. It can take a long time to teach the horse this, but it is worth it because it improves his balance and shape. Using the inside hand incorrectly is a quick fix, but it is also a dead end.

I advise riders to practice exercises such as making the circle bigger and by doing shoulder-in. Watch yourself: when you feel the horse falling in on the inside shoulder, what do you do? Are you using the inside rein against the neck? Or do you yield your horse out from your inside leg? If you do the latter, you will be able to maintain a much nicer flow, relaxation and balance in your horse.

What to Do with That Outside Rein

There has been a lot of confusion among riders about what to do (or not to do) with the outside rein. Many riders that I meet have learned to ride the horse 'on the outside rein'. Often this is interpreted as keeping the outside rein short and keeping the horse (too) straight. This interferes with the bending and suppleness of the horse. On the other hand, riders that overwork their inside hand and do too little on the outside create too much neck bending in their horses which causes them to fall over the outside shoulder.

When the goal of your training is to make your horse supple through gymnastic exercises and then to collect the horse, you first need a horse that can bend to both sides evenly. When it can bend evenly, you can straighten it. In this context straight means with hips and shoulders aligned. Bended exercises are necessary to conduct the power generated by the hind legs through the body in a biomechanically correct way. When the shoulders are in front of the hips, no matter if the horse is on a straight or on a curved line, the energy can flow from back to front. It creates a balanced, supple horse that can move elegantly. The suppleness is achieved by bending the horse to both sides, stretching the muscles along the spine. With a stiff horse, that is why in the first instance we focus only on the inside rein (bring the nose in) and the inside leg (hollow the inside of the horse's body). We alternate this by often changing the direction to the left and right. Consider a stiff garden hose with some kinks in it. Bending it gently to the left and right makes it supple and smooths the kinks. Then we can shape it in a curve and let the water flow through it easily. Any kink would block the flow.

Now, when the horse can bend around your inside leg, sometimes you will notice that the bend is getting too much and the horse is breaking out over the outside shoulder. Now here is the job for the outside rein: to reduce bending when it gets too much and to guide the flow of energy around the bend toward the mouth of the horse and into your hands. When the horse bends too much in its neck, it is as if the garden hose has got a kink. The power of the hind legs gets partially lost over the outside shoulder. The outside rein smooths it out. You bring the outside

of your body through the curve by allowing your ribs and shoulder to move forward. And by touching the outside shoulder of your horse with the outside rein, you place his shoulders inward, in front of the horse's hips.

It is important that the horse understands how to bend correctly around your inside leg. In that case the inside leg can turn the outside shoulder-in. If the horse does not understand the inside leg, the inside leg aid will make the hindquarters fall out.

If you start using your outside rein before you have bending, you limit the amount of suppleness and flow that your horse can develop. The outside rein is both a reducing and guiding rein. Do not reduce or guide something that is not there! An outside rein that is too short, or an outside hand working backward will keep the horse stiff and prevent his back muscles from becoming supple. That is why in the Art of Riding we work in phases. In the first phase, with a stiff horse, we work on the inside leg and inside rein to achieve bending and suppleness. Only in the next step do we reduce and guide with the outside rein. When we can bend the horse only from the seat, then we leave the inside rein alone and guide the horse only from the outside rein.

One pitfall is that people sometimes get stuck in the first phase, pulling the inside rein and bending the neck of their horse too much. So, in the end, the outside rein is the most important! However, not every horse can start with it. That is why often we need to start with phase 1, the inside rein and leg. But always keep the end goal in mind: a horse that is supple and balanced and can bend from your seat. Start using the outside rein as soon as you can to guide your horse through turns. Distinguish between the direct rein (placing the head) and indirect rein (placing the shoulders). Only use the outside rein as a direct rein when the horse bends its neck too much. Otherwise, use it as an indirect rein to place the shoulders in front of its hips (guiding the horse). This allows the energy to flow freely from the hindquarter into your hands.

Trotting with Your Nose

How do you ask your horse to transition from walk to trot? Would it be weird if I share with you that I trot my horse from the movement in my nose? But it is true, I do. And I ride my trot transitions from collected trot to extended trot and back to collection from my nose too.

When I want to transition from a walk to a trot, what I really want is to change the rhythm of the walk into the rhythm of a trot. Picture the spine and rib cage of the horse as a pendulum. What I want is to change the three-dimensional swing of the horse's spine by influencing the pendulum at the right moment. If I touch the pendulum with my seat or legs at the wrong moment, I block its movement. I restrict the three-dimensional swing of my horse's spine. If I catch the pendulum at the right moment, I can positively influence the energy and swing of the pendulum. I can change the three-dimensional swing of my horse's back from walk to trot.

I can do this by changing the rhythm in my seat: by moving my seat bones and hips faster. A well-responding horse will follow my movement almost immediately and pick up his own rhythm to match mine. However, there is always a delay between my increase in rhythm and the horse's response. There would always be a brief moment where we are working against each other and my seat bones and hips are not moving together with the horse. This is unpleasant for the both of us. I don't like to teach this to students because it takes time to train the horse to respond properly. The 'moving against each other' moment takes too long in the beginning. So, instead, I let my hips follow the current movement. I stay in the 'now', together with my horse. I am always following what is there in my hips. I start the increase in rhythm somewhere else. My preference is my nose, but it could also be in the ankles or the back of the head. When that part of my body starts to increase in rhythm my sensitive horse that is tuned into my seat and rhythm will automatically pick up his own rhythm, match it with mine and start trotting. It is the same with transitions within the (sitting) trot. The amount and speed of the movement of my nose determines the length and rhythm of the horse's steps.

When we follow the movement of the horse's back, our hips lift and drop in the rhythm of the horse's hind legs. When the horse's ribcage gets lifted, so does our upper leg (thigh). On the other side, the rib cage swings down and our leg drops. Because the belly of the horse swings to the left and right, we have a lift and drop in the horse's spine, the horse takes us forward, and the movement in our seat becomes three-dimensional. This movement gets into all parts of your body. When I ride a walk or sitting trot and my head is relaxed, balancing on my neck. The movement of my horse travels up my spine and into my skull through the occipital joint. This makes my head move in rhythm with the horse. Even the tip of my nose follows this movement. My nose, almost invisible, moves up and down and left and right, drawing a little figure eight in the air in front of me. Also, my legs swing down in the horse's rhythm, which is especially easy to feel on a bareback pad on a well-moving horse. When we free our ankles and ride without stirrups, we can feel how even our feet swing in little figures of eight. When we follow the movement of the horse, we swing in his rhythm. When we want to change the movement, we need to change our movement. But my butt is always the last thing to change, as that is the part that is physically connected to my horse. I don't want to do something the horse is not doing, as that means going against the movement. Instead, with the rest of my body I guide the movement to what I want it to be and my hips follow when my horse responds. My hips continue to follow the horse. They stay in the 'now' and ride what is there.

The difference can be very subtle in a good rider with a sensitive horse. Your change and the horse's change will happen practically instantaneously. So it is hard to decide where the change starts. In your hips or somewhere else? But in a not-so-advanced rider and/or horse it is very clear. When we start by changing the rhythm in the seat and the horse does not follow, we see riders pushing into their horse's back. Or we see people pushing with the lower leg instead. But any time we feel we have to push a non-responding horse forward, we will find ourselves tensing somewhere in our body. We block the swing of the pendulum, because we catch it in the wrong rhythm. That does not help to get a horse forward. So, instead, see if it benefits you to free your head and ankles and increase the movement from there. Feel how the pendulum

in the spine of your horse makes your entire body swing. Increase this swing with your nose and/or ankles. It's almost like 'bobbing' your horse from walk into trot. If your horse does not respond, kiss (lightly squeeze) your lower legs but stay in the rhythm. That means, NOT with both legs at the same time, but left/right in the swing of the horse's stomach. Is that not enough? Apply a small tap with the stick just behind your leg to explain what you mean. But even the tap with the whip needs to be in the correct swing of the pendulum and it should never stop the movement in your body. Your neck and ankles stay free. Your nose continues to swing. Stop your body and you stop the back of the horse from swinging. Keep your body free and in rhythm with your horse, and then see if you can guide the walk rhythm into a trot rhythm. Pick up the walk into a trot. And let it start in your nose. See what happens!

THE BIOMECHANICS AND
TRAINING OF THE HORSE

Preconditions to Training

It is normal for us to prepare properly when we decide to start a new sport. Take running. We decide that from now on, we plan to run twice a week. We go to the sports store and buy ourselves proper running shoes and maybe even a fancy watch that can monitor our distance, speed and heart rate. We ask the shop assistant for advice and try out different shoes to find the pair that fits us best. We all know that our training will be uncomfortable and more likely to fail if we go for the wrong shoes. We also know that we should follow a training schedule to gradually increase the distance we can run. If we have a physical problem, we will adjust our training schedule accordingly.

However, with horses, many owners seem to believe that meeting all the proper preconditions to successful training is not that relevant. Is it because when we run without following the proper preconditions such as fitting shoes, we ourselves are the ones that suffer? And with our horses, as most of them suffer in silence, we can choose to ignore these preconditions with excuses such as 'limited funds' or 'he doesn't seem to mind'? Imagine having to go to school each day on an empty stomach, or having to sit at your desk doing your work on a chair with nails sticking out of the seat into your delicate behind. You would not be able to focus on your work, now would you? The same goes for our horses.

For me, before training starts, it is important that for both my own horses and my students and their horses, we meet all the preconditions to successful training. These include: teeth care, hoof care, feeding, housing, social contact, regular vet checks and properly fitting tack. It basically means the horses should be free of any kind of stress. The Art of Riding is all about 2-way communication, about building a relationship with your horse, about two bodies and two minds working together in harmony. How can we ever achieve harmony with a horse that has a stomach ache from chronic ulcers because he is never allowed outside his box and gets fed 5 kg of concentrated food each day? Or with a horse in pain because of an ill-fitting saddle or a jaw that can't move properly because his teeth are neglected? Therefore, I always

engage in a conversation with my students about these preconditions when they come and train with me. I want to check the tack that they are using and sometimes, I have to advise them to change something. Instead of feeling disappointed that something isn't right, most of my students are grateful to get this information so they can take action to improve their horse's well-being and optimize their training. You can't help not knowing about things you haven't learned about before, so there is no personal blame to anyone who rides with an ill-fitting saddle or with neglected teeth on a horse if they believe (and often are told by their expert saddle-fitters and equine dentists) that everything is alright. But there is blame to put on those who know things aren't right but who still go on in the same way.

Sometimes I encounter people who have a horse, acknowledge they have a problem with bad teeth or a poorly fitting saddle, but then tell me the horse has to deal with it, because it will be sold anyway, or because they have no more money in their bank account. Would you deal with poorly fitting shoes and still run in them, even if they hurt your feet and give you blisters or ruin your knees? If you have the means, you will buy better shoes. If you can't afford that, you may have friends that can lend you another pair of shoes or in a worst case scenario, you would rather stop running than ruin your feet. Why not do the same with your tack, for instance? If you know that your saddle doesn't fit and hurts your horse while you ride, no matter the excuse, simply don't use it anymore. Borrow another saddle, ride bareback or simply train your horse from the ground until your circumstances change. There are always solutions for those that look for them, but there will never seem to be a solution for those who are not really willing to change.

Here is the reality if you want to have a horse and train with it: you have to start addressing all of the preconditions first. When people ask me for advice about buying a horse, I always stress the point that buying the horse is not the biggest issue. The biggest things are to get it vet checked, to purchase proper fitting tack, arrange for a dentist and a good hoof trimmer and to find suitable stabling for the horse with turn-out and social contact. The responsibility never stops. Training only starts

after you have looked into all these preconditions and concluded that your horse is free of pain, stress and frustration.

Most of the time, the horses that come to me for training because of behavioral problems improve simply by being housed in our Paddock Paradise, with the balanced, stable group of horses that we have here. There they get a better education in manners [from the other horses] than I could ever do in the same time. They get to move as much as they like and play with and groom other horses. People are amazed by how well-behaved their horses are when they come home again. Well, these people will have to make sure to keep up with the preconditions like turn-out, social contact, movement and healthy food, and then, the chances are that their horses will stay that nice will increase tenfold. Good training is only the icing on the cake.

Make yourself familiar not only with the training aspect of horses, but with all related topics that can influence the welfare of your horse. A horse that is stressed, in pain, hungry or annoyed cannot learn! Proper feeding, feet, teeth and equipment are necessary for proper training. Do not just trust the experts when they tell you something. Make sure you understand WHY and WHAT when you speak with experts and always ask for a second opinion if your gut feeling tells you something isn't right. But most important, never make ANY excuses to justify the continuation of something that you know is bad for your horse. Change it! Your horse is under your care. It is your responsibility. If you want him to work with and for you, make sure he can, optimally.

The Development of Balance

With a young horse or a horse that is very out of balance, I would recommend training him from the ground until the horse has reached a level of balance and self-carriage to keep a healthy and soft posture. The same applies to the unaligned and unbalanced human. The horse-and-rider combination is a delicate balance, and if one or both of the individuals is out of balance, the combination will definitely not be in balance.

The Academic Art of Riding offers a great training system of groundwork, lunging and in-hand work to prepare horses for riding. The work from the ground teaches the horse how to balance his body, it makes the horse more symmetrical in his body and it teaches the rider feeling and timing without disturbing the horse with her weight. It also enables the rider to establish a communication with her horse from the ground that can be transferred to riding aids later on.

Only after this level has been reached should the horse be ridden. In the ideal case, that means that the young horse can keep a horizontal balance and the rider can stay perfectly vertical in their own body use. Of course there are exceptions. Some horses will drop the back when the rider sits on them or throw their weight forward. Also, with longer rides on a young horse it will be too much to stay with your seat bones in their back for a long time. In these cases, I recommend a light seat (See 'Wag your Tail') where the rider comes out of the back of the horse with the seat bones and brings the spine in a more diagonal direction, forward and upward. This takes some of the pressure off the horse's back muscles and allows the horse to release the upper line and stretch forward-down. The rider should still follow and allow the movement of the spine of the horse.

When a horse can remain in a horizontal balance, the rider can remain vertical. That is the ideal 'normal' position for horse and rider. In this balance, the horse can maintain rhythm and from here, can extend and collect. The rider can then start to use the spine (or a specific part of

the spine) as leverage: bringing the weight slightly back to collect or slightly forward to send the horse forward-down.

It is important that the forward or backward movement of the rider's spine keeps the alignment. Sending only the rider's stomach forward will result in an arched back, which will make the knees pinch. Bringing only the stomach back too much will result in a too-rounded back and a slumped posture in the rider, which presses the lumbar part of the horse's back down and reduces the swing and the upward thrust. Quite often, it should be more thinking than doing, as doing is in most cases already too much.

Using the spine as a leverage to move the point of weight can only be done on horses that are able to follow the point of weight of the rider. In other words, they must be physically able to collect or go forward-down to the extent the rider is asking and they must learn to understand the meaning of this shift of weight in order to respond. Slowly, the spectrum of extending and collecting grows larger, as the horse develops the bend of his hind legs and the strength in his muscles and the rider develops sensitivity in her seat. Over time, this will lead to more advanced exercises such as half-steps, piaffe and canter pirouettes. The stronger and more bendable the horse gets from behind, the more he can balance his body weight on the hind legs. This means the horse needs to develop the carrying capacity of the hind legs and learn to bend his joints. The maximum collection is in the levade, where 100% of the body weight of the horse and rider is delicately balanced over the horse's hind legs for several seconds.

The Movement of Horse and Rider

To allow our horses to move, we need to understand how they move and how they move us. Let's explore the movement of our horse.

The engine of our horses is in their hind quarter. The hind legs move the horse forward. The hind legs have angled joints and big muscle groups. This allows them to bend and stretch, and to push out backward, push (stretch) upward and step forward under their bodies. The movement of the hind legs has three phases: the forward swinging phase, the carrying phase and the backward pushing phase. With each stride the horse goes through all three phases. The forward swing is the phase of the stride in which the hind leg swings forward after leaving the ground, then lands under the stomach and the horse puts weight on it. Then, the body of the horse starts to move over the standing hind leg. The hind leg is carrying the weight of the horse and lifts its back and chest. When the hind leg has come behind its hip joint, the leg goes into the backward pushing phase: the horse pushes himself forward over the standing leg. Which phase of the hind leg is more dominant determines the body use of the horse, or the other way around: the body use of the horse determines which phase of the hind leg is more dominant.

When the forward swing and the carrying phases are more dominant than the backward pushing phase, the hind leg swings far forward under the point of weight of the horse, his pelvis drops, making the tail come down. Then, this forward standing, carrying hind leg lifts the horse's chest and shoulders. When the backward pushing phase is more dominant, the hind leg steps further out backward, tilts the pelvis the other way, making the tail come up and the back of the horse drop. The horse brings his weight more to the front legs and the under neck is visible.

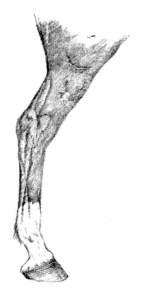

The movement of the hind legs brings the spine in a three-dimensional movement called 'schwung' (swing). This schwung consists of lateral flexion (bending), axial rotation and vertical flexion. When the forward swing and carrying phases are more dominant, this makes the spine swing such that the back comes up and the horse's ribcage swings down on the side of the carrying hind leg. This allows the rider's hip and leg to go down on the side where the hind leg comes forward. The ears of the horse move forward with each stride (toward the hand). When the backward pushing phase is more dominant, the back swings down, the horse's ribcage does not rotate as much or can even rotate in the opposite way, making the rider's hip come up on the side where the hind leg moves forward. The ears of the horse move up with each stride (against the hand).

The movement of the horse starts in his hind legs and is transferred into his spine through the sacroiliac joint. The three-dimensional movement travels up the horse's spine all the way to the head, where the movement comes out through the movement of the skull. You can imagine that if we blocked the movement anywhere, we would create brace and friction in the horse's joints. In the short run, this leads to discomfort and lower quality of movement in the horse. In the long run, it can lead to permanent damage to joints and tendons and to behavioral problems

in the horse. Blocking the movement can (unconsciously) happen when riders are stiff in their own hips. This prevents the three-dimensional swing of the spine. Another way to block the movement is by fixing the horse's head in a certain position. This is done when riders hold the reins too tightly and do not move their hands in rhythm with the horse's head. It also happens when using fixed reins. As soon as the horse cannot move his head, the three-dimensional swing in his spine is blocked and friction occurs in the horse's spine. To get out of this discomfort, the horse will drop his back and pelvis.

Our own movement while riding starts in our pelvis and upper legs. Our hip joints should be supple to follow the three-dimensional swing of the horse's spine. This movement travels down our legs and up into our spine. The movement comes out of our feet, hands and the top of our head. If we stiffen just one joint somewhere in our body, this will interfere with the movement in all other joints. Ever tried to shake your hand with all fingers relaxed versus with your little finger stretched out? Now imagine that applies to your entire body and you will understand that all joints should be moveable at all times while you ride. Stiffening somewhere will lead to increased friction and shocks in your body, usually the spine. This can cause back pain, neck pain, sore shoulders and headaches. Not to mention the decrease of movement this gives to the horse, with similar discomfort as a result.

Riders who have only ridden stiff-backed horses teach their pupils that this upward movement of the seat bone or no movement in the seat at all is the way it should be. These riders will train their horses accordingly, thus creating a non-swinging back. I find it important to explain to my students where the movement originates, how it should feel and to teach the rider the proper gymnastics for the horse's back to allow more suppleness and schwung.

In walk and sitting trot, the horse's rotation of his spine causes his ribs to lift and drop alternately. So while the left side of his ribcage drops down due to the belly swinging to the right and the left hind leg coming forward under his body, the right side of the ribcage is lifted. This creates a bilateral vertical movement in the rider's upper legs, causing

the hip joint to open and close. One leg is lifted and at the same time, the other leg is dropped. This alternate lifting and dropping of the legs, combined with a bit of left-right swinging, travels up the rider's spine and crosses diagonally over to the opposite shoulder of the rider through the solar plexus. This is the 'spiraling spine'. The movement comes out the top of the head, which causes the head to move with the occipital joint freely and supple. You can see the result in a slight movement of the rider's nose.

Imagine walking in place, without lifting your feet from the ground. Your knees go forward and back, in a soft bend. One after the other. The hips and ankles do the same, causing one leg to bend more while the other is stretching and vice versa. My favorite exercise to teach sitting trot is to have my students do this on a mini-trampoline, as it gives a them the best upward 'lift' in the movement. When you practice, feel how the movement travels up your spine and comes out the top of your head.

In canter, the hind legs of the horse do not move in the exact opposite rhythm and the vertical flexion of the horse's spine is the biggest. There is more of a rounding and stretching over the horse's spine. The movement in the rider's inside hip can be described as a backward circle, where the outside hip joint is moved forward a bit earlier than the inside hip and doesn't really circle but rather moves forward, up and back. The movement is transferred through the arms into the hands, which follow the same backward circle the inside hip makes. The movement also transfers through the spine, coming out the top of your head. Because both hips do not move the same in canter, it is a difficult movement to feel and analyze in the seat. My advice: just relax into it , keep your hip joints free and let the horse carry you forward in canter.

You must be able to follow the movements of the horse before you can start to influence them. That is why you first need to be a good passenger before you can start to shape your horse and change things for the better. Most of us do not take sufficient time to establish a good following of the movements, and rush directly into trying to take charge.

To learn to first feel and follow the movement of the horse makes the rider aware of the hind legs. Seat bones, hip joints and legs, all moving in rhythm with the horse's back, give the rider an awareness of where the hind legs are at all times (the left hind leg swinging forward; the left seat bone, hip and leg of the rider moving forward and down, the right hind leg pushing over the ground; the right seat bone, hip and leg of the rider moving backward and up). After the rider can follow the hind legs of the horse, the rider can start to take control of them. For example make the forward swing of the hind legs bigger by emphasizing the forward-down swinging movement of the seat bones, hip and leg. A leg aid just at the moment before the hind leg is leaving the ground makes the backward push of the standing hind leg smaller. The following of the horse's movement that the rider's body is doing does not just come through the seat bones, but through the entire pelvis, the hip joints and upper legs, so that even in a light seat when the seat bones do not touch the horse's back, the rider can follow the movement of the horse's back.

There are many ways to teach the rider to feel and follow. As a test of whether the rider is able to feel the hind legs, I ask my students to tell me when a certain hind leg is in the air. They learn to feel their own body and notice when their seat or leg drops. So, again, it starts with becoming aware of what is happening in your body and in the body of the horse underneath you. Notice, follow and then influence where necessary.

This Thing about Collection

Most recreational riders are not that concerned about the concept of collection. It is something only dressage riders need, to score points in the dressage ring. Nowadays it is often associated with stressed horses, horizontally pulled curb-bit shanks and swishing tails. This of course has nothing to do with collection. And the ability to collect your horse correctly is what every rider needs in order to keep a riding horse healthy and balanced.

Without training, all horses carry more body weight on their front legs, which have mostly straight joints that are not very good at absorbing shocks. In addition, as riders sit closer to the shoulders of the horse than their hind legs, this presses the chest down between the shoulders. A horse moving in natural balance will add the rider's weight to the front legs. These fragile support pillars are not used to supporting that much weight at higher speeds. Normally, the horse leans over the front legs while grazing. More weight on the front legs at higher speeds increases the impact of legs slamming into the ground, harming the joints and tendons.

Therefore, we have to do something with the horse's natural balance to avoid over-straining the front legs. We have to influence the horse's natural balance, teach it to shift its weight back and carry us on forward-stepping hind legs, which can be used as shock absorbers with their angled joints and large muscle groups.

We can train the hind legs to step under the horse's point of weight from the ground. When we ride, we can ask the horse to do the same, using our seat and additional aids. We cannot force a horse to bring his weight onto the hind legs. We can invite him to do so, if he is capable. We don't need to collect our horses up to piaffe to keep them healthy, but each rider (no matter in what discipline), should strive for horizontal balance. This is when the horse has neither more weight on the shoulders ('downhill') nor more weight on the hind legs ('collected' or 'uphill'). Of course, the more collected the horse can move, the less strain there is on his front legs.

On a horizontal horse, the rider can be in vertical balance: her spine is vertical compared to the ground and compared to the horizontal spine of the horse. The angle between the horse's spine and the rider is 90 degrees. This 90 degree angle is a rule of thumb that can be followed at all times and in all stages of training. In a horse that moves more downhill, the point of weight is shifted forward and the rider should bring her own point of weight over the horse's point of weight, thus leaning slightly forward toward a light seat. In a collected horse, the point of weight shifts back and the rider should bring her own point of weight back. The advanced horse and rider will use the rider's spine as leverage: by shifting forward or back the rider moves her point of weight, inviting the horse to follow with his own point of weight, thus collecting or riding more forward-down.

One cannot sit collected on an uncollected horse. However, many instructors seem to believe that if they teach their students to sit 'collected' the horse will automatically follow. This may be true for those riders who have already experienced the feeling of true collection and thus know what they are after and for those horses that have the physical ability to collect naturally. However, it is my experience that for most riders and most horses, a 'collected' seat does not automatically lead to a collected horse. In fact, often a rider that sits too heavily will have the opposite effect on the horse: it will press its back away and push out backward with his hind legs. To collect your horse, you need to prepare your horse sufficiently and not aim for the end result right away.

However, to always remain in the light seat will also not bring us any closer to collection. We can use our seat to play with the point of weight and move it slightly forward or back. Over time, as the horse learns to follow our point of weight and gets stronger in his haunches, we can move the point of weight more and more back toward collection. Awareness and feeling in your seat for the horse's balance, relaxation and suppleness is what we need to play with the point of weight. This is something that the rider will develop over time.

To Bit or Not to Bit

Bits are one of many discussion points among horse lovers. Do we need them?

There are those who claim it is not possible, ever, to control your horse without using a bit. To those people I'd like to say: control is not force, control is not achieved through pulling an animal in the mouth. Control, if you want to use that word, is reached through understanding and communication.

Then there are those that say that it is not 'natural' to put a piece of metal in a sensitive mouth, and therefore bits should never be used. To those I say that, in that case, we should not ride horses at all, as it is also not natural for a horse to have a rider on his back. A lot of harm can be done by using a bit incorrectly. I have seen terrible things done to a horse's mouth; from bloody and cut mouth corners, to splintered bars, damaged teeth and scarring inside the mouth. However, it is also possible to severely damage a horse's head using a rope halter, cavesson or any other tool on the nose bone. I have seen broken nose bones, excessive scarring on the nose from 'serretas' (cavessons with a pointy bottom) and terribly wrong doing with hackamores. Even without anything on the horse's head, we can do tremendous harm by conditioning horses to move in a certain shape, or by not shaping them at all.

So, in my opinion, the topic should not be the type of tool ("mine is better than yours"). Let's have a sound discussion about how tools should and should not be used. A rein, connected to the horse's head in whatever way, whether to the mouth or nose, should NEVER be used in a pulling way, there should NEVER be force placed on the horse's head. Any tool that influences the skull can do massive damage when used wrongly. Not only the damage I mentioned above, but also damage to the horse's esophagus, windpipe, tongue bone, salivary glands and neck vertebrae.

Another reason why one should never pull on the reins is a biomechanical one: When a hand works backward and the rein pulls on the horse's head

or mouth, it compresses the horse's spine. This compression works its way back through the spine into the pelvis and results in a flattened pelvis and hind legs that are pushed back and out. In turn, this creates a bigger forward push in the horse, which in most cases is then caught again in the rider's hand, which has to pull harder, and so on. In short; it does not work to pull on the reins to stop or control a horse. Actually, pulling has the opposite effect. That is why in racing, you see the riders pull on the reins. It creates a 'pushing' speed. Unfortunately, it also creates a 'spectacular' extension in the front legs and it gets awarded high scores in too many competitions, both in dressage and in gaited competitions. This way of extending the gaits damages the front legs and stiffens the back and is in no way a harmonious or natural way of moving.

In the Art of Riding, our aim is to work the hind legs forward under the point of weight and allow the horse to carry us in a balanced, healthy and harmonious way, with movement that adds beauty to the natural gaits. For that, the pelvis needs to tilt, bringing the tail down. This does not work when we pull, that just pushes the hind legs out and back creating the opposite effect

What we strive for is a horse that seeks a giving hand. This does not mean there is no contact. Our definition of contact is simply lighter than many other trainers. For many, contact equals weight. For us, weight equals the wrong biomechanics. Contact should be subtle, should be vibrations, should be energy, should never be strong, never be fixed, always forward. That is why in the Art of Riding, you can see sometimes slightly hanging reins. This does not mean that there is no contact, horses can still feel our half halts and vibrations through the reins, and we can still feel the horse. You can imagine that using a bit like that, or a cavesson or a hackamore or whatever bitless bridle, has a different effect than using strong contact with tight reins.

Here is how I like to use my tools: With a young horse, I prefer to start without a bit. I use a cavesson on the nose. I use this tool, because it has a direct influence on the skull and into the spine. Snaffle bits and many bitless bridles influence the lower jaw, which is moveable. I like the

lower jaw to be placed correctly by the horse itself. When I ask with a direct cavesson rein for a horse to look to the left, when his nose turns left, his lower jaw is free to move to the right, aligning the molars on the right side of his jaw. This is what the Dutch call *stelling*, or correct bending at the poll. It creates freedom between the jaw and the atlas vertebra. When I ask the same with a snaffle or a bitless bridle that crosses underneath, I actually pull the lower jaw to the left, which can result in a tilting of the head, a stiffening in the jaw or a wrong rotation into the horse's spine. With the cavesson, I teach the horse the direct and indirect rein, my half halts, the stops. I bend the horse and send him forward-down toward a giving hand.

When I am ready to ask for more collection, I add the curb bit. The curb is an unbroken bit with shanks. The curb works through the leverage system of the shanks and the chin chain. The curb (when used correctly) stretches the muscles in the upper line in the neck, causing the ears to move forward and the skull to be placed more vertically with an 'open neck'. Meaning, the space between the jaw and the atlas should be kept 'open' so that the horse's biofunctions remain intact. A snaffle cannot do this, as it does not have this leverage system and would simply pull the lower jaw closer to the neck, compressing the windpipe, salivary glands and esophagus.

Many consider the curb to be a cruel tool and a snaffle bit more friendly. Snaffles are widely accepted in the horse community. However, with the snaffle there is far more risk of compressing the neck and damaging the bars and teeth. Many riders ride with lots of weight on the snaffle reins. With a curb, you already have a good communication with a loose rein. Yes, it looks more scary with the shanks, but as with any tool it is not that scary once you understand how to use it. Many of the Old Masters would only use cavesson and curb and you can find many pictures of them riding with a loose rein. That is the beauty of the curb; you have communication with a very loose rein and you can stay very quiet and soft in your hands. Of course, the image of the curb nowadays is a bit different, as we see many riders abusing the curb, riding with tight contact and shanks pulled backward vertically.

An alternative for the curb for those who do not want or cannot use a bit is the hackamore. It uses the same principle of the leverage through the shanks. Nowadays, we even have a combination of cavesson and hackamore available: the cavemore. The downside of a hackamore is that when you use the reins, it closes the horses mouth and in some horses that creates a stiffness in the jaw.

So, for a long time I train my horses with the combination of cavesson, for bending and half halts, and the curb for collection.

When my communication with my horse is good enough, when my horse understands me through my seat and when my control over my seat is precise enough, I can stop and turn my horse in the correct bend and with the right forward-down movement just from my seat. Then, I no longer need to use the cavesson and can ride with the curb only. As the curb is unbroken, you cannot use your reins separately. Therefore, the curb should be used one-handed. When my seat becomes even more advanced and my horse can collect from the seat, I can take it all off and ride without anything on the head.

This should always be the goal of the Art of Riding; to master the seat and the communication with your horse to the degree that you do not need so many tools. However, very few riders have sufficiently precise control over their seat right from the beginning. And very few horses instinctively understand what we mean and can execute all exercises without some extra support. For most horses, we need these tools, whether a cavesson, curb, snaffle, hackamore or other bridle, to clearly explain what we want from the horse.

For those riding naturally, with no contact to the head, the topic is what kind of communication you can have with your horse and how subtle and nuanced you can make this conversation. Can you ask your horse to place its jaw in the exact position to allow good biomechanics? Can you truly free the shoulders? If you can: great! Keep going! You don't need tools you don't need!

For those riding with tight contact: is your horse truly stepping forward under and bringing up the back? Is the jaw flexible and the mouth soft? Can you ask your horse to place its jaw in the exact position to allow good biomechanics? Can you truly free the shoulders? Is your horse in balance? You can only test this by taking the 'side-wheels' off. That is why I frequently leave the bit out to see if I can get the same results without.

Both 'extremes' probably want the same result; a horse that can move freely, feels good about itself and sits comfortably. But by fighting over the tools and not questioning their use and how we could learn from each other in finding a way to reach our goals, we will not resolve our issues. In both worlds, I see good trainers and bad trainers. All the good ones have in common that they can communicate with their horses and give them a biomechanically correct shape.

In this whole discussion, let's not blame the screwdriver for doing a bad job. Let's blame the handyman who is using it in the wrong way. Any device on a horse's head will be as severe as the hand that holds the reins! In my opinion, we should treat bits and all types of bridles as tools to communicate with our horses, to be replaced by our seat when our communication improves.

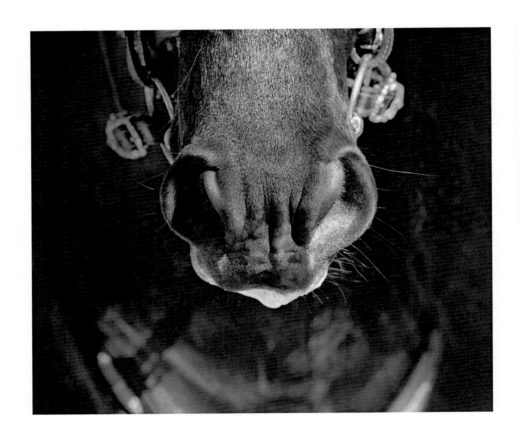

Six Important Factors to be Effective in Your Communication with Your Horse

We communicate with our horses using signals, both while riding and in working our horses from the ground. In the horse world these signals are also known as aids. The word aid implies, correctly, that it is a signal that is supposed to help your horse. That it is there to improve something, whether it is his posture, balance, speed, shape or direction. The most common known aids are the seat, legs and reins while riding. But also the whip and voice can be used as aids. While working from the ground, we can use the lunge line or lead rope and body language as aids. So we have a whole scale of signals that can help us communicate with our horses in order to help them perform better.

If an aid does not help, because whatever you applied made your horse get out of balance, on the forehand, out of rhythm or stiff, then aid obviously did not 'aid' your horse. It did not help him get better but made him worse. Or, if your horse does not respond to your aids and ignores them, so nothing changes after you have applied your signal, you are not communicating with him and can't aid him. In these both cases, basically, your aids were not aids, but mere signals that did not work or not the effect you intended.

But how can we make sure our aids are most effective?

1. Have a plan: know the what, how and why

Ok, so you want to communicate with your horse and help him improve in his groundwork or riding. You want to do dressage or other kinds of exercises. Or you just want to be able to tell your horse in what direction to move and at what speed. Basically, every horse you want to handle needs some basic training and therefore, everyone handling a horse needs to have a basic communication in place to tell the horse what to do. If you don't want to train a horse in any way, then stay out of the field, don't go near and just observe them from a distance. As soon as you get closer, you need to have some basic language. Even if it is just to ask him to back up a step so he can get his hoof off your toes.

The more advanced you get into dressage exercises, the more advanced and nuanced your language with your horse will be. Subtle weight changes in your body will invite the horse to collect and extend, a gentle increase of the rhythm in your body becomes a transition. The dance becomes ever more subtle and complex.

When you start with basic training, you don't need to understand the subtle weight changes that can become a piaffe. But you need to understand the what, how and why from the signals you are applying on the level you are at. Everything you want to ask your horse, you ask with a signal. Can you specify each separate signal you use? Do you understand what exactly you want your horse to give you in response to every signal? Do you have a good reason why you want your horse to respond to you like that? For me, the why should give me an answer that explains how I can build the next exercise out of the one I am doing right now? So, how can moving the shoulders bring me a step closer to a half-pass? How can backing up bring me closer to collection? Know what you are working with and why. And, most importantly, do you know exactly how to apply your signal in the clearest way for your horse? Elements 2 to 6 will help you with just that.

2. Educate your horse

When we start to apply aids, we create a language between ourselves and the horse. This language is new to both of us. The horse must learn the language. He must understand what we mean by the aid we give. We need to teach the horse the appropriate response to our signals. The horse needs to have had his basic education, explaining the signals to him, before we can use these signals to do exercises. Which signals you choose to teach your horse and what exercises you want to come out of them in the end depend on the choice of your path with your horse and what discipline you are in. Important is to realize that the horse must learn your signals and see them as aids. That means you have to treat your horse as a student and educate him. Education means explanation, motivation and feedback. You can teach a horse signals in many different ways. There are many methods for teaching a horse. I don't intend to write in favor or against any of them. Whether you apply your traditional pressure and release, clicker training or other

ways of positive reinforcement, whether you teach them your legs and reins while sitting on a youngster or introducing them to him from the ground, it all boils down to your skills as a trainer to be able to educate the horse in responding to your signals. And that is exactly what many horse owners and trainers overlook: that it is not only the reward in the case of an appropriate response or the increased pressure applied when a horse is not responding. The core of the matter is: How clearly can you pose your question to the horse? How good a teacher are you? How well did you manage to explain to him what answer you were looking for?

3. Timing

It is easier for the horse to respond to your signal or question when he not only understands what you want, but when you apply the aid with the right timing for the horse to actually DO something in response.

Riders often ask their horses to do something at a moment when it is impossible for the horse to do it. Then the only option the horse has is to ignore the aid. If this happens often enough the horse will learn to disregard the aid altogether. The classic example from the Academic Art of Riding is this: if you ask the horse to step its hind leg further forward under his body, the horse can only respond to this question when he is lifting his leg. When it is free of weight. The weight needs to be on the other hind leg. If you ask a horse to step under with a hind leg when he has that leg on the ground and his weight is fully on it, you make it physically impossible for the horse to respond to you in that particular moment. That may teach the horse to ignore your question and disregard your aid.

4. Intensity

The next thing to consider is: what if you know what you want, your horse is educated, your aid is clear, your timing is right, and nothing happens? Then, you may have to consider repeating the aid with a higher intensity. I work in a buildup of three steps. In groundwork for example, I would (1) point with the stick to the body part I want my horse to move, (2) gently tap it and (3) tap it in the intensity needed for the horse to respond. This is considering my horse already understands

the aids and is just a bit slow in his reaction. In the phase where I explain to the horse what my aids mean (the education phase), I may choose another approach, based on the character of my horse. But considering he knows it, the 1-2-3 method is what I usually apply to get a quicker or bigger response. If you apply the same aid ten times with an intensity or energy that is too low to make the horse respond, you end up pushing him every step, but just getting slower and slower. The horse will disregard your aid. You are nagging him all the time with no result. If you approach it with the buildup of 1-2-3 you may have to wake up the horse with a three maybe once or twice, and from there on you may only need a 1.

5. Visualize the result

All of this makes no sense if you have no clear idea of the desired outcome in the back of your head. You should know and visualize and even feel in your body what it is you want to have happen. Then, your mind and body work as one. You will send out a consistent, clear message to your horse. Being unsure, doubting yourself, changing tactics ten times in one minute, this all this leads to confusion and to most horses sort of blocking out their trainer. It also means that once you ask a question, you should be sure you know that the horse can answer (he understands what you mean and your timing is right) and that you know you can follow through (you can go up in intensity). You already see what you want to happen. Anything else is out of the question. This puts your entire body and soul behind your signal. Your body will change even if you don't think about consciously doing anything in your body. It will make your question crystal clear.

6. Stop in time

Maybe the most difficult of all is knowing when to stop or reward. Especially when the horse is still learning the language and has not fully grasped the meaning of your aids yet. We often ask for too much and don't see the little responses of the horse that is thinking in the right direction. Therefore we do not release pressure, or we reward or otherwise reinforce too late. We continue to ask for something bigger, instead of rewarding the horse for being on the right track. Then, the

horse may stop trying his best, because we have overlooked his attempts. He will lose his motivation to try hard for you. To have developed the eye and feel to know when to stop, even if it may not look like anything has changed in the horse yet, and to allow those tiny responses of the horse to grow bigger over time, as the horse's confidence in his answers grows, that is the true skill of the good trainer.

When a trainer is aware of these key factors his communication becomes clearer, he is truly able to aid his horse to a higher level of performance. The horse's understanding of the aids can develop rapidly and save us not only time, but many moments of misunderstanding that can be frustrating for us and our horses and can even lead to dangerous situations sometimes. So, know what you want, be clear, educate your horse, improve your timing and intensity and make sure you stop and reward in time. Happy training!

Playing With Focus, Relaxation and Energy Using Materials

In the Academic Art of Riding, we take the training of horse and rider very seriously. In order to develop to a higher and higher level, reach more collection and ride the advanced exercises, we need to train regularly with a well thought through program and a decent training schedule. In this elegant dance between human and horse that we strive for, we require the utmost concentration, openness and connection between horse and rider. We work with small nuances. We play with balance, rhythm, tempo, the position of the shoulders and the hind legs, the shape and suppleness of the horse. And ultimately we want this all to flow effortlessly from one exercise into the next. For this to be the most harmonious and elegant dance we need a certain lightness, a certain playfulness. But in our daily training, while working diligently on mastering the techniques and developing our horse's body in strength and suppleness and overcoming our own physical limitations, we can get stuck in a rather hard focus. Our daily training is not effortless. It is blood, sweat and tears. And that is how everyone starts when learning something new. But getting stuck in practicing the same things over and over until they are perfect, or getting stuck in focusing on what is still not OK in your training will make you and your horse lose the fun and will sometimes block you from further progress. It can give you hard focus. Hard focus means that the mind may be focused, but is not relaxed. You may have energy, but no grounding. You may have technique, but no balance. The opposite of hard focus is complete relaxation without any focus. Then, you will be stuck in the same snug comfort zone forever. Repeating what goes well. It feels great, but there is no progress.

Progress comes when you can combine your focus with relaxation and energy. With a relaxed, open mindset, you can focus without getting hard. For this relaxed, open mindset you need to get out of your comfort zone but in a way that you and your horse build up positive experiences. That is why I alternate my training days. I have days in which I train within our comfort zone, when I do not make any attempt to take the next step. I have days on which I push the boundaries. Then there are days on which we just relax, and days on which we play. You can

combine these things too! Play and moving boundaries go very well together. The best combination is to work on finding a balance between focus and relaxation at a higher level of energy!

Finding a balance between serious training and play is important. It helps put things in perspective and brings a smile into your day and that of your horse. It helps to overcome things that are difficult, by approaching them from a completely different perspective.

I like to add playful elements in my training workshops and in my lessons. Quite often, when I see one of my students getting too serious, I soften them up by using materials. I give them a certain task, something to focus on outside their own bodies and the body of their horse. I use it for myself too. I find myself quite often in my comfort zone repeating the things that are already going quite well. To get myself out of my comfort zone and to give myself a clear focus, I use materials to set out a certain task for myself and my horse. A task that is just one step outside my comfort zone. A task that, when successfully completed, has helped me make my comfort zone bigger. It has expanded our boundaries. Then, I can continue to ride the same exercises in this expanded comfort zone until either I or my horse get a bit bored and unfocused again. And then I think about the next step up and how to reach that next level. And then I usually get creative with materials again.

Lately, my goal has been to ride my appaloosa, Fitzer, in a relaxed canter to the left and right. Canter has never been his 'thing' and the right canter was actually non-existent. When we started to introduce the right canter again, he was physically able to do it, but mentally he got very stressed. So the first goal was to reach mental relaxation in the right canter. Simply by doing it a lot and after each canter do some basic exercises that are inside his comfort zone to find his relaxation back. The next step, when this worked, was transitions. Riding all transitions, while keeping a relaxed mindset. Picking up the energy and bringing it down. It helped tremendously to improve his relaxed focus on me. He got attentive, quick on the aids, while keeping his cool. When we could also include canter in this work, I got a bit stuck in this part of our comfort zone again. We could do a nice forward canter, nice transitions,

keep our cool and ride bigger and smaller circles in canter, with some collection and extension. But what's next? Any idea of continuing more collection or riding more exercises in the canter led to a lack of motivation on my part and some inner stress on his part. So I came back to using materials.

The exercise was very simple. Inside my 20mx40m arena, I created a rectangle, of about 25mx12m. On one of the long sides of this rectangle, I put some soft poles in two parallel lines, thus creating a straight line, like a tunnel, between the poles. The other long side was the wall of my arena. Then, I made the four corners with cones. Corners with inside and outside cones, to make clear 90 degree corners. First in walk and trot and then in canter, the goal was to ride in this smaller 'arena'. To make clear turns in each corner and ride a straight line on a longer rein between the soft poles on one long side and ride the shoulders a bit away from the wall and back again toward the wall on the other long side next to the wall.

The result? Left canter? Piece of cake! Right canter? We missed some turns to begin with but managed to do the same as on the left rein in the end. This resulted in a super relaxed and confident horse that started to think for himself, looking for the openings between the cones and the soft poles, that straightened up between the poles and that collected beautifully in each turn. And a focused yet playful rider who was not cramped in her body to do everything right, but simply focused on the next turn or straight line and let her horse and her body do the job.

Materials give us focus. Both the rider and the horse can see where they need to go. The material helps to frame the horse, so that the rider can do less with her aids and relax her body. For exercises that are new for the horse and/or the rider and that ask something from the horse that is still physically difficult, the rider can sometimes get a bit stuck and cramped from trying to frame the horse with her legs and reins. Materials can take over part of the job and make life easier for horse and rider. Then, when the exercise is understood and the horse knows what to do with his body, we can take the material away and let the rider guide the horse.

Materials also give us a very easy way to measure success. You either stayed between your cones, soft poles or whatever you used, or you did not. Also our horses understand this success and often become quite motivated to find the right way through the materials. Any failure should not be taken too seriously. Oopsie, is usually what comes out of my mouth. Simply try again, give the horse time to discover what is expected and go slower if it turns out to be too difficult. Any success is usually followed by a huge shout of joy from the rider anyway. Believe me, that happens naturally.

The playfulness the material can bring to any serious rider is fantastic to watch. We all love to play sometimes, and in play we do things we would not have imagined doing without the material. The material gives our mind another goal. "Simply make that 90 degree turn in canter" instead of "Let's try a quarter-canter pirouette now." In the second phase, I start to think "Oh my god, I am not sure if I can collect my horse so much without him stiffening up." I want to do it perfectly. It makes my mind block my body. It cramps me up. But simply taking the turn, not micromanaging the horse, gives me a feeling of that perfect quarter-canter pirouette that I can take with me on the day that I train it without material.

The ultimate effect? The materials take our focus off the details in our body and the horse. It brings fun to the work. And it gives us the relaxed focus we want in ourselves and our horses with a higher degree of energy and collection than we could have ridden without the material. Thus it helps us pave the road to that next level in our riding. It gives us a taste of the next step. Of more straight, more collection or more energy, whatever you are working on at that point. This taste of the next step, this experience of the horse straightening more, lifting his back more, collecting more, this feeling is what we can then remember the next time we ride without material. It also gives us the confidence that yes, our horses and we ourselves can actually ride that exercise! The confidence it brings in horses and riders is fantastic to experience.

Enjoy playing!

About the Author:

Ylvie Fros is a Centered Riding® Level III instructor, squire and selected trainer in the Academic Art of Riding as well as a bodywork practitioner. She teaches around the globe to promote healthy dressage for horses in combination with increased body awareness for riders. Ylvie has studied and continues to study with experts in horse and human biomechanics, Zen and the Academic Art of Riding.

Each year she hosts courses with her teachers such as Bent Branderup, Tom Nagel and various Centered Riding® instructors. At her stable in the Netherlands she trains her own (rescue) horses in the Academic Art of Riding and teaches students from around the world and from all different disciplines and backgrounds how their bodies and minds can make the difference in their riding. Her mission is to spread awareness for horse-friendly training methods and at the same time assist riders in developing their own bodies and minds to their maximum potential so that they can become the best riders, trainers and people they can be.

"I live to develop my mind, my body and the mind and body of my horses, and am passionate about passing my knowledge and experience on to other horse lovers. I combine my knowledge of teaching, the use of the human body through Bodywork and Centered Riding® and training horses with the Academic Art of Riding by Bent Branderup® as a full package for the development of horse and rider. I believe that the insights that Centered Riding® and the Academic Art of Riding have to offer are beneficial for all types of horses and riders in all disciplines. I teach a highly diverse range of students all over the globe, from advanced dressage riders to western riders and recreational riders. With a new perspective on the training of the horse, the seat and the relationship between human and horse, there is something in this training approach for everybody." -Ylvie Fros

XENOPHON PRESS LIBRARY
www.XenophonPress.com

Xenophon Press is dedicated to the preservation of classical equestrian literature. We bring both new and old works to English-speaking riders.

30 Years with Master Nuno Oliveira, Henriquet 2011

A New Method to Dress Horses, Cavendish 2018

A Rider's Survival from Tyranny, de Kunffy 2012

Another Horsemanship, Racinet 1994

Austrian Art of Riding, Poscharnigg 2015

Classic Show Jumping: the de Nemethy Method, de Nemethy 2016

Divide and Conquer Book 1, Lemaire de Ruffieu 2016

Divide and Conquer Book 2, Lemaire de Ruffieu 2017

Dressage for the 21st Century, Belasik 2001

Dressage in the French Tradition, Diogo de Bragança 2011

Dressage Principles and Techniques: A Blueprint for the Serious Rider, Tavora 2018

Dressage Principles Illuminated, Expanded Edition, de Kunffy 2019

École de Cavalerie Part II, Robichon de la Guérinière 1992, 2015

Equine Osteopathy: What the Horses Have Told Me, Giniaux 2014

Fragments from the writings of Max Ritter von Weyrother, Fane 2017

François Baucher: The Man and His Method, Baucher/Nelson 2013

Great Horsewomen of the 19th Century in the Circus, Nelson 2015

Gymnastic Exercises for Horses Volume II, Eleanor Russell 2013

H. Dv. 12 German Cavalry Manual of Horsemanship, Reinhold 2014

Handbook of Jumping Essentials, Lemaire de Ruffieu 2015

Handbook of Riding Essentials, Lemaire de Ruffieu 2015

Healing Hands, Giniaux, DVM 1998

Horse Training: *Outdoors and High School*, Beudant 2014

I, Siglavy, Asay 2018

Learning to Ride, Santini 2016

Legacy of Master Nuno Oliveira, Millham 2013

Lessons in Lightness, Mark Russell 2016

Methodical Dressage of the Riding Horse, Faverot de Kerbrech 2010

Military Equitation: or, A Method of Breaking Horses, and Teaching Soldiers to Ride, Pembroke, *and A Treatise on Military Equitation,* Tyndale, edited by Charles Caramello, 2018

Principles of Dressage and Equitation, a.k.a. Breaking and Riding, Fillis 2017

Racinet Explains Baucher, Racinet 1997

Science and Art of Riding in Lightness, Stodulka 2015

The Art of Riding a Horse or Description of Modern Manège in Its Perfection, D'Eisenberg 2015

The Art of Traditional Dressage, Volume I DVD, de Kunffy 2013

The Ethics and Passions of Dressage Expanded Edition, de Kunffy 2013

The Forward Impulse, Santini 2016

The Gymnasium of the Horse, Steinbrecht 2011

The Horses, a novel, Elaine Walker 2015

The Italian Tradition of Equestrian Art, Tomassini 2014

The Maneige Royal, de Pluvinel 2010, 2015

The Portuguese School of Equestrian Art, de Oliveira/da Costa 2012

The Spanish Riding School & Piaffe and Passage, Decarpentry 2013

To Amaze the People with Pleasure and Delight, Walker 2015

Total Horsemanship, Racinet 1999

Training with Master Nuno Oliveira double DVD set, Eleanor Russell 2016

Truth in the Teaching of Master Nuno Oliveira, Eleanor Russell 2015

Wisdom of Master Nuno Oliveira, de Coux 2012